TILL DEATH
DO US PART

The true story of misguided love, marriage, death and deception

Published in 2005
by Maverick House Publishers,
Main Street, Dunshaughlin, Co. Meath.
www.maverickhouse.com
email: info@maverickhouse.com

ISBN 0-9548707-8-6

5 4 3 2 1

The paper used in this book comes from wood pulp of managed forests.
For every tree felled, at lest one tree is planted, thereby renewing natural
resources.

Printed and bound by Bercker, Germany.
The moral rights of the author have been asserted.

A CIP catalogue record for this book is available from the British Library.

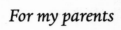

For my parents

ACKNOWLEDGEMENTS

I would like to thank a number of people for their help and support with this project. Firstly thanks to Mary Whelan's mother Marie Gough for her time and patience. Also to Valerie Hanley and Darren Boyle for their invaluable assistance. I would also like to thank all the journalists who I work with in the Four Courts in particular my boss Diarmaid McDermott.

Siobhán Gaffney

CHAPTER 1

Colin Whelan was a methodical killer. He had spent months planning his crime and rehearsing the murder and his alibi. There would be no unforeseen problems on the chosen night of the killing. More than anything else, he knew his victim wouldn't scream with fright or summons help when he walked into her bedroom to kill her because the victim was his wife of just six months.

Whelan decided to go through with his plan on the night of Wednesday, 28 February 2001.

His motive was money. A year earlier, he had taken out a £400,000 (€500,000 approximately) insurance policy on his wife's life. He also wanted to begin a new relationship with a Welsh woman he had met over the internet.

He maintained his composure throughout the day in question and gave away no clues as to what he planned. He left his office at Irish Permanent on St Stephens Green at 5pm to catch a train home. He was so casual he even read the *Evening Herald* as he travelled to his home in Balbriggan.

He had spent the previous seven months trawling the internet for information on how to commit the perfect murder. He had typed in the word 'asphyxiation' followed by 'loss of consciousness' and 'how to asphyxiate' to learn about death.

~ ~ ~

During the course of the day, Whelan slipped out of work to purchase a gift for his wife. He bought a cast-bronze figurine of a man casting a fishing line from a boat, entitled 'A Day's Fishing' in Brown Thomas. It matched a similar piece they had received as a wedding present.

When he returned to his desk that afternoon, he spent 30 minutes on the phone to his online girlfriend, Helen Sheppard, arranging to travel to

Wales later that weekend. When he finished the conversation, he next rang his wife at her place of work while at the same time searching the internet for information on 'loss of consciousness'.

When he arrived home at 6pm, he changed clothes and left for the Body Lab gym, leaving his wife to prepare his dinner.

His wife, Mary Gough, was in good spirits. She had told friends at work that she was going into Drogheda town that evening to collect the results of a blood test from a homeopath in an attempt to lead a healthier lifestyle. She wanted to attend a detox programme to lose weight and she was looking forward to it.

Whelan spent an hour in the gym before returning home. After they had both eaten, he drove her to Drogheda where she had an appointment at 9.15pm with her homeopath, Michael Hughes, who noticed that she was in good humour that night.

Whelan gave away no indication of what he had in mind. When the couple arrived home, he told his wife that he was going to take a shower and he walked upstairs.

Oblivious to her husband's psychosis, Mary Gough spent some time attempting to work out her new detox programme before going upstairs to prepare for bed.

She was attacked moments after she had changed into a pair of white, teddy bear patterned pyjamas in the master bedroom of the couple's new home.

There was nothing to suggest that anything was wrong. Her husband simply walked into the room, took his wife by surprise and started choking her to death.

Mary hadn't a chance. She stood just 5ft 4 inches in her bare feet while Whelan towered over her.

A mixture of sheer strength and surprise gave him the advantage. As he entered the bedroom, he gripped the cord of a dressing gown in his right hand. Standing a few inches behind his wife, Whelan grabbed her from behind without warning and grappled with her neck.

Attempting to fight her husband off, Mary summoned all her energy and turned around to face her husband, probably staring at him with terror stricken eyes.

In stunned disbelief, she tried to break free from her husband's forceful grip but as she flayed her arms in the air, Whelan's hold on her neck became stronger and stronger. She could barely breathe.

In an effort to pull his hands free from around her neck, Mary scraped her nails down her husband's bare chest. This caused him to relax his grip temporarily. For a moment she was able to breathe and took a huge lungful of air. She then made an effort to run but Whelan grabbed her left arm while she tried to get free, ripping the left sleeve of the pyjama top just above the cuff. The tear extended almost all the way around the sleeve, such was the force he used.

Maddened, Whelan grabbed his wife's long, brown hair and dragged her onto their king-size bed. Mary kicked to fend him off and screamed at him to stop but he wouldn't. Whelan was not listening, but was transfixed by his sickened mission.

Pulling the cord from his dressing gown free, Whelan took his wife's head in his hands and first wrapped a towel around her neck, followed by the cord. The towel, Whelan had researched on the internet, would disguise ligature marks left by a manual strangulation. He hoped this would make it difficult for detectives to identify the cause of death. As she continued to scream, he pulled the cord tighter and tighter. Mary's face soon began to turn blue and the first trickle of blood oozed from her nose.

In a desperate effort to save herself, she scraped Whelan down his chest once more. This gave her a few moments grace from the relentless stranglehold he had around her neck.

Wiping the blood from her face with her right hand, she tried to escape but was unable because she was too weak. Her face had now turned from blue to purple and her breathing had become laboured.

Sensing that her death was imminent, an enraged Whelan pulled the cord with such force that Mary bit her own tongue. Unable to scream anymore, Mary resigned herself to her fate.

She was going to die at the hands of her husband. When she lost consciousness, Whelan removed the cord from her neck. His young wife was now paralysed and dying. He then looped the cord around his dressing gown and tied it.

Like a rag doll, Mary was then dragged from the bed by her killer. Holding her two limp arms, Whelan pulled her across the house landing and down the stairs, head first; thud, thud, each time her back hit a step.

Halfway down the stairs, Whelan accidentally dropped her right arm. She was still clinging to her life and tried desperately to grab hold of the side of the wall in a final bid to stop her husband. But he just pulled her harder down the stairs.

When he reached the bottom, he laid his wife out on the floor and stared down at her.

Incapable of speech, she stared back at her husband of six months and cried in silence. She could feel her breathing getting shallower. Whelan sat in the dark, watching his wife lose consciousness as her life slipped away. He waited and waited until she passed out.

No one knows if he spoke to Mary as she lay there dying. He probably went through what would ensue over the next few days. He wanted her family to believe the death was an open and shut case of his wife having fallen down the stairs.

After half an hour, Whelan climbed over his dying wife's broken body and went upstairs where he retrieved the quilt from their bed and a yellow towel from the main bathroom.

On his return, he wiped the blood from Mary's mouth and nose before placing the hand towel around her neck. He then placed the quilt over her freezing body to keep it at room temperature. This was a premeditated murder. Whelan had studied the modus operandi of the American serial killer

Henry Louis Wallace, who kept his victims warm to disguise the time of death.

When the time was right, at 12.16am, he dialled 999 and asked for an ambulance.

It was time for him to play the part of the distressed husband. His emergency call was connected to ambulance control at Tara Street in Dublin city.

'Hello, fire and ambulance,' answered the controller.

'Hi. Hi, I need an ambulance, my wife's after falling down the stairs,' he said, whilst pretending to cry.

'Okay, how far did she fall?' the controller asked.

'Right from the top.'

'What's your address please?'

'49 Clonard Street, Balbriggan.'

'Clonard Street?'

'Yeah, Clonard, Balbriggan,' said Whelan

'Okay, is she conscious?'

'I don't think so. What can I do? I don't think she's breathing,' answered Whelan.

'You don't think she's breathing?'

'I don't think so.'

'Okay,' said the controller.

'What do I do?'

'Where is she now, is she flat on the floor?'

'Yeah.'

'Okay, well what you need to do, okay, try not to move her neck, open her mouth, get down and look and listen and feel is she breathing,' said the controller.

Whelan pretended to kneel at his wife's side and try to save her life. Sensing that something terrible had happened, the ambulance controller dispatched an urgent message to all medical teams in the area, seeking assistance.

'Lads, will you get your Swords ambulance there, we've got a POS. Lady fell down stairs. She mightn't be breathing. Balbriggan. Clonard Street.'

Whelan listened patiently and didn't panic, though he did pretend to cry at one point during the conversation.

'Hello sir,' the controller asked. 'Is she breathing?'

'I don't . . . hold on, hold on,' said Whelan.

'Hello sir. Can you see her chest moving?'

'I don't think so; she's bleeding really badly from her nose or something,' said Whelan.

'Okay, can you see her chest moving up and down?'

'Hold on. No, no,' said Whelan.

'You can't?' asked the controller.

'No, I can't.'

'Okay, open her mouth. What age is she?' asked the controller.

'Twe . . . twenty-seven.'

'She's twenty-seven?'

'Yeah,' said Whelan.

'And you definitely can't feel air coming up against your face.'

'I can't. I'll put my face down, hold on, I'll do it. No, I can't,' said Whelan.

'She's not breathing?' asked the controller.

'No, I don't think so.'

'Okay, open her mouth, okay, and close off her. Pinch her nostrils with your other hand.'

'Yeah,' said Whelan.

'Okay and blow into her mouth. Is the air going into her sir?'

'Yeah,' replied Whelan.

'Could you see her chest rise and the air going in?'

'Yeah but there is nothing.'

'And okay can you feel a pulse, can you check, just go to where her Adam's apple is on her neck, okay. Just slide your fingers down on the inside of it and see, can you feel a pulse?' asked the controller.

'I don't think so, I don't know whether it's me own or what, I don't think I can feel anything,' said Whelan.

'You don't think you can feel anything?'

'No,' answered Whelan.

'Right, so do you want, do you know how to do CPR at all?'

'Kind of, half like . . . I've seen it, I don't know.'

'Okay, what's her colour like, is she . . . ?'

'She's blue,' interuppted Whelan.

'She's blue?'

'Well, she's going really . . . yeah,' said Whelan.

'Okay, what you need to do is blow air into her, okay? So, close off her nostrils and blow air through her mouth, okay?'

'Okay, right,' said Whelan.

'Is the air going in?'

'No, hold on, no, I . . . sorry, I have to get up and . . . '

Whelan left the phone go silent for a minute to make it appear that he was desperately trying to revive his dying wife. When he said that he could find no pulse, he was told to administer a heart massage. He pretended to do this while on the phone to the emergency services.

'Hold your two hands together, okay, pull your fingers back up and put the heel of your hand right in the centre of her breastbone, not too far down, not too high up but right in the middle of her breastbone,' said the controller.

'Right,' answered Whelan. 'Okay. And push, is it?' asked Whelan.

'And push and you want . . . hello? . . . hello sir? . . . hello?'

'No, there's nothing happening,' said Whelan.

'Okay, what you do okay, you press down about one and a half inches 15 times and then you go back and you blow into the mouth,' said the controller.

The emergency services prioritise their calls. As Whelan acted out the part of a stunned husband whose wife was dying, ambulances were scrambled to the scene in the hope that someone could save the victim's life. The operator stayed on the telephone line, instructing Whelan how to perform CPR. The more he spoke, the more the operator began to panic. All the killer could say was that she was now purple in colour and that she was bleeding from her nose.

'Try and help her breathe. So once again, you've got to breathe into the mouth twice. Okay and make sure the air is going in. Open her mouth, pinch off her nostrils with your hand and blow in a long hard breath for three seconds,' instructed the controller.

'Do I keep doing this?'

'Yes, so blow in for three seconds. Okay, let her exhale then and blow in for another three seconds and then start CPR again. So remember, don't go too far down the breast bone, use the heel of your hand, go down about an inch and a half. Okay sir . . . okay sir, any joy? . . . is she breathing at all? The ambulance is on its way sir. We also have a fire engine on the way out to you, okay. They should be there in a minute, okay? We need you to keep breathing into your wife, okay. Stay with me on the phone, I need you to keep on breathing into your wife.'

Whelan gave the same response. He said nothing was happening.

CPR causes a specific muscular movement when administered. When first-aid and mouth to mouth resuscitation is given, it causes the patient's chest cavity to fill with air. It is clear that Whelan never intervened to save his wife's life because he constantly said her chest didn't move. At one point during the emergency call, the operator told him to check his victim's mouth to see if something was blocking her air vent.

'Is there anything in the back of her neck you can scoop out with your finger or anything in the back of her throat,' asked the controller.

'Nothing, I checked her tongue, her tongue is fine,' answered Whelan.

'Her tongue is fine, okay, blow in twice again . . . okay, and then start and then press down on her chest 15 times an inch and a half,' said the controller.

At this point, an ambulance crew entered 49 Clonard Street. It was 12.30am and the medics found Mary lying at the bottom of the stairs with her husband asking the same question over and over again. He asked, 'Is she gone?' repeatedly.

They knew immediately that something sinister had happened. One of the paramedics observed that if Mary had indeed fallen down the stairs she would not have landed in the position she was found. She was too neatly tucked in beside the stairs; her legs were together and straight. It was as if she had just collapsed while standing in the hallway.

They also knew that Whelan had not performed CPR on his wife. Mary's head was angled towards the front door, making it uncomfortable for such a tall man like Whelan to perform mouth to mouth.

Her head was not tilted back, her mouth was closed and her airway had not been opened. Anyone trying to perform CPR in this position would have instinctively turned Mary's head to a better angle.

There was another clue. Whelan had no blood on his face. If he had attempted CPR on Mary, it would follow that he would have had blood on his face as she was covered in blood coming from her mouth and nose.

Whelan had done nothing.

They also wondered why Whelan had covered her body with a quilt. At no stage was he told to cover his wife with a quilt as it was not a priority in the management of cardiac arrest.

One of the ambulance crew also observed that Mary was cold to touch but the house itself was warm. She was noticeably cold.

When the crew first arrived at the house, it was just 15 minutes after the accident had been reported. Years of experience in dealing with life and death had taught the paramedics what to expect. They thought Mary would have been warmer given there was no major blood loss, which could cause a reduction in body temperature.

As the paramedics pulled back the quilt that covered her body, except for her outstretched arm, they found a blood soaked towel covering her neck. They knew that something murderous had happened. Their suspicions were further aroused by Whelan.

He hovered around as they attempted to revive Mary, desperately hoping that she would not be saved. Indeed, as the paramedics worked on his wife as she lay unconscious on their living-room floor, Whelan coldly asked, 'Is she dead?'

CHAPTER 2

Mary Gough was the second youngest in a family of six children and was the only daughter of Marie and James Gough. They lived in the small village of Stamullen in Co. Meath. Although she was doted upon by her parents and brothers, she was not spoiled. On the contrary, she was a very independent and outgoing woman. From her early childhood she had a special relationship with her mother Marie. The two women rarely, if ever, argued and were more like sisters. No matter what happened, they were always honest with each other. It was the type of relationship that many parents long for.

The relationship grew noticeably stronger after Mary's father died unexpectedly in 1989. At the time, Mary was aged 15. The death had a strong impact on her. She found her own strength in dealing with the tragedy and became even more independent-minded. Being the only girl in the family, Mary learned to speak her mind and wasn't afraid of saying what she thought. And with her inner strength established, she then harboured a desire to become financially independent. She began working when she was 16, as much to establish her own independence as to earn money.

Her mother remembers her first job in the nearby town of Drogheda, which is located eight miles from Stamullen. Rather than ask anyone for a lift to work, the young Mary cycled to work if there wasn't a bus.

'There was no stopping Mary,' her mother recalled.

On Mother's Day in 1991, Mary took a job as a bar girl in the Huntsman Inn which lies in the centre of Gormanstown in Co. Meath. The bar was less than two miles from the Gough family home. She was still attending school but loved the work. She juggled her paid work and school work without problems.

'Even though she didn't like school, she still went. I remember the last day she was doing her Leaving, she came home and lifted the lid of the bin and dropped the bag into it,' her mother laughed fondly.

Two years later, in 1993, she met her future husband in the same bar. She was 19-years-old at the time and Whelan made a strong impression on her. The two knew each other to see but were not well acquainted when they met.

Whelan came from a similarly well-respected family of three brothers and two sisters. He came from Gormanstown where he lived with his parents, Andrew and Olive Whelan. Nothing marked him apart from his contemporaries. He had never shown any violent or psychotic tendencies as a teenager and had never been in any sort of trouble.

On the contrary, he was very much a young man who applied himself to his studies, which had secured him entry into Letterkenny College in Co. Donegal where he studied computers. After graduating in 1992, he got a job as a computer analyst with Irish Permanent in St Stephens Green in Dublin city. The position was considered a major coup for a young graduate.

The Huntsman Inn was Whelan's local pub and was close to the family home. When he was introduced to Mary, he had a broken leg. He sustained the injury while attending a REM concert at Slane Castle. Physically curtailed for that summer, he decided to spend much of his time in the Huntsman Inn.

He didn't ask her out until the following Christmas when he summed up the courage. There is no doubt that she was thrilled. Whelan was tall, handsome and regarded as a good catch by Mary and her friends.

The relationship was casual at first but nevertheless, Mary brought him home on St Stephen's Day before the young couple headed off to Funderland in Dublin city. Marie Gough vividly remembers meeting Whelan for the first time.

'Colin drove a blue Ford Fiesta and was working in Irish Permanent at the time; he was 22. He seemed a nice lad and I knew Mary was very fond of him.

'They went off to Funderland in the RDS. Mary had a great time; she won an awful lot of soft toys and I still have a bag of them in her room.'

Whelan struck Marie Gough as a perfect gentleman and she grew fond of him.

'He was well-mannered. He called me Marie. I treated him as a son; the lads treated him like a brother.'

The relationship soon became serious. Whelan spent money on Mary, often buying her jewellery and roses. He also made a point of ingratiating himself with Marie. The young couple would often take their parents to shows or concerts.

For the first few years Mary and Whelan seemed to be in a stable and loving relationship. But in April 1995, on an otherwise normal evening, he abruptly ended the relationship.

'He was handing her a cup of tea,' recalled Marie, 'when he just turned around and said it's all off—just out of the blue. She was in an awful state and he was so cold.'

Mary returned home in floods of tears. By this time, she was very much in love with Whelan and had privately planned to marry him. She got such a shock that she vomited minutes after she came home. What upset her more than anything was that Whelan had given her no explanation. She couldn't comprehend his coldness and ability to withdraw emotionally.

She was devastated. When she woke the following day, she wouldn't get out of bed. She was heartbroken.

Her mother, though, had seen it coming. Days earlier she had noticed Whelan acting strangely in her home. Every time her daughter made an advance on him, he would pull back.

'I got the impression he did not want her,' she said.

Another incident had happened the night before Whelan ended the relationship when he telephoned looking for Mary. Marie answered the phone. When she told him that Mary had gone out with friends, Whelan became unusually angry.

Days later, Marie telephoned Whelan herself. Her daughter was genuinely upset and had started blaming herself for the break-up. She wanted to see if she could do anything to help, or possibly even get the two to talk.

'I decided to ring Colin to see the reason for this break. But Colin was aggressive to me. I said to Colin on the phone, "Why did you break it off with Mary, she is here in a terrible state." But he just said, "It's not my fault, she's like that."'

Marie was struck by his coldness and detachment. This would become one of Whelan's most distinguishing features in the years to come.

However, Mary soon rediscovered her independence. In the weeks that followed, she landed an exciting job as a secretary with a film company who were promoting the film, Rob Roy. At the premiere of the film, she was photographed with the actor Liam Neeson and also appeared on television.

The film company were impressed with her organisational skills and attention to detail and offered her a full-time position. To accept the position, they asked Mary to move to Scotland where the company planned to film a motion picture, but she wouldn't go. Although she wouldn't admit it to anyone, she wanted to resume her relationship with Whelan.

Instead, she joined a solicitors firm called Wade's, who were located in Swords in north county Dublin. She joined the practice as a receptionist before moving into conveyancing work. It was around this time that she began to meet up with Whelan again. Six months after the split, Whelan and Mary resumed their relationship. Only this time, the relationship she entered into was far more serious.

It was clear to anyone who knew them personally that marriage was part of their future plans. Marie was happy as long as her daughter was happy.

In August 1997, Whelan bought his grandfather's house at 49 Clonard Street in Balbriggan, Co. Dublin. This was a shrewd financial move for a man of his age. At the time, Mary was just 23-years-old and wanted to settle down. She decided to pack her bags to move in with her boyfriend of five years, leaving her mother and the family home in Stamullen.

The young couple were the envy of their friends and acquaintances. They had their own home, independence from their parents and good careers. Nothing, it seemed, could hold Whelan and Mary back.

Then their lives were shattered when Whelan killed a 62-year-old woman in a driving accident. The victim was his neighbour, Elizabeth Murphy.

Whelan had been drinking in the Huntsman Inn that evening and decided to drive home when the accident took place. Mary had met him in the pub and decided to follow him in her own car.

Elizabeth Murphy was travelling as a passenger with her husband Thomas, when they came upon Whelan who drove straight towards their car.

Whelan decided to swerve to avoid the car but it swerved simultaneously, causing both vehicles to smash into each other. The victim died as a result of the injuries she sustained in the crash.

Whelan was rushed to hospital but had suffered no serious injuries. But that was not the end of the matter. Whelan was charged with dangerous driving and causing the woman's death. He was lucky. The State decided not to proceed with the charge of drink-driving.

The accident brought the couple closer. They became inseparable. Mary became an emotional crutch of sorts for Whelan. They now lived together and were husband and wife in almost every sense.

Whelan formalised their living arrangements when on 9 October 1998, while on holiday in Fuerteventura, he surprised Mary by producing an expensive four stone diamond engagement ring. Mary never took the ring off and always wore it. After their engagement, Whelan told everybody they would be getting married in two years but Mary would have married him immediately; she idolised him.

The only thing that could interfere with their plans was the pending court case. The death impacted on Whelan, but not to the extent that one would imagine. He never fell into a depression over the death or stopped driving. If he had any emotional guilt about what happened, he never showed it.

When the trial came up for hearing at Trim Circuit Court, Whelan decided to plead not guilty even though the evidence was weighted against him.

In evidence, Garda Desmonde Lambe described how he had attended the scene of the crash, which occurred on a straight stretch of road, where the surface was dry. He recalled how he had gone to Our Lady of Lourdes Hospital in Drogheda where he found Whelan wearing a surgical collar.

The jury found Whelan not guilty on the drink-driving charge. The other charge of causing death by dangerous driving was withdrawn by the DPP at the last minute, when they offered no evidence.

His trial judge Raymond Groarke said, 'The accident occurred as a result of your driving and it was something you will have to live with for the rest of your life. Nothing would be served by sentencing the defendant to a term of imprisonment.' However, he was found guilty of careless driving and was fined £350 and banned from driving for six months, even though one of the investigating gardaí told the court that he smelt drink on his breath and his eyes were bloodshot after the crash. Whelan had gotten lucky.

~ ~ ~

In April 1999, Mary and Whelan moved out of their house in Clonard Street while it was being renovated and stayed with friends in Balbriggan. The house was given a complete overhaul. They installed a new kitchen and modernised the two storey house before their planned wedding.

Mary was very house proud and had stylish taste. The renovation was a success and considerably increased the value of the property.

Marie would often stay with her daughter and Whelan in the months leading up to their wedding. The young couple even gave her a room. Mary bought a wardrobe and a chest of drawers and put them in one of the new rooms for her mother.

The couple tied the knot on 9 September 2000 in Mary's local church in Stamullen, which is only a couple of hundred yards from her family home. Whelan was not a typical groom: he helped his fiancée to organise every aspect of the wedding. He accompanied Mary and her mother to every meeting and appointment to do with the wedding, including collecting the cake.

'He was everywhere. The only place he didn't go with her was when she was choosing the dress and I don't know how he didn't manage that. He even came with us to collect the wedding cake; at the time I thought that funny,' Marie recalled.

Privately though she sensed that something was wrong. She dared not say a word to her daughter for fear of causing upset or offence but her instincts told her that something was not right. She now believes that her daughter had second thoughts about the marriage.

'I have a feeling that she didn't want to marry him and that's why he was around so much. He wanted to make sure she couldn't be on her own with me. He was afraid that she would confide in me. Even when she would drop me home, he would always come with us in the car. She'd never come here without him. She came once but he never stopped ringing her on the mobile,' she recalled.

When the day finally arrived, Marie was nervous. She found Whelan to be cold and calculating, although not openly. She couldn't understand why she didn't like Whelan or found him untrustworthy, but she did nonetheless.

She remembers her daughter's wedding day vividly for this reason and the fact that it ran like clockwork; it was almost regimental.

'I had a bad feeling about it; something was wrong. It should have been the happiest day for me but there was something cold about it. There was something I couldn't put my finger on. It must be mother's instinct but Mary didn't look a happy bride. You know the way you would normally see couples; they would be grinning at each other. No, there was none of that; everything was formal. When I think of it now, everything was for show; there were no outwardly shows of affection at all.'

Marie believes her daughter was deeply unhappy about something. But this remained unspoken: a guarded secret by Mary. After the wedding ceremony in the small church in Stamullen, Mary and Whelan, like all newly-wed couples, stood outside to greet and celebrate with their family and friends. This was supposed to be an occasion of great happiness for the 26-year-old; she was finally marrying her boyfriend of seven years; the man of her dreams. But standing with her new husband shaking her friends' hands, Mary suddenly broke down in tears. Knowing that people would see her cry, she ran back inside the church and began shaking and crying uncontrollably. She was followed by her bridesmaids and family but her husband stood outside.

Marie recalled, 'She started to cry, she got very, very upset. She couldn't stop crying. She was in there for ages. He was outside and it seemed as if he couldn't care less, I couldn't get over it.'

The Gough family didn't suspect that Whelan was the source of the problem. At the time, they suspected that Mary had become upset because her father was not there.

After a while, Mary composed herself and rejoined her husband who was chatting to their wedding guests outside the church as if nothing had happened. Then the two of them posed for their wedding photos.

Looking every inch the radiant bride, Mary smiled at the camera. She never did tell her mother what really upset her on her wedding day but Marie can now only guess what made her daughter cry.

After the wedding, the couple went on honeymoon to Singapore and Thailand. That holiday was supposed to be a once in a lifetime journey across south east Asia. It was supposed to be a journey where they would plan out their lives together. Instead, Mary returned to Ireland a changed woman. Gone was the independent woman and straight talker. Her mother was the first to notice the change.

~ ~ ~

The most obvious change in her character was her attitude to her mother. Mary stopped inviting Marie to stay in her house for no apparent reason. However, Marie was more perturbed by her appearance. Her daughter had started dressing in dowdy, old clothes. Whenever Marie arranged to meet her daughter, Whelan would also always turn up unexpectedly.

'Things changed for Mary when she came back from her honeymoon. It was not immediately noticeable but after they got married I was never asked to stay at 49 Clonard Street overnight. Also, Mary would say to me, "We will go for lunch?" or go shopping or that but it would not materialise. It was not that Mary was any busier, she was becoming distant.

'Mary stopped wearing perfume and make up which was unbelievable for her. She also stopped wearing nice clothes and dressed casual which was unusual if you knew Mary. We never went shopping after Mary got married, something we always did before.'

There was nothing Marie could do. While she firmly believed that Whelan had instructed his young wife not to communicate with her mother or socialise with her, she put her suspicions to the back of her mind. She discarded her fears as needless worries and constantly reassured herself by saying that Mary was happy and content. But as time passed she became more convinced that something was wrong. In her heart, she felt that Mary desperately wanted to talk to her about Whelan but was too scared. Her fears grew as the days and weeks passed.

'I noticed the week before Mary's death, she rang me every evening, which was unusual. I felt there was something she wanted to tell me but she could not.'

Something else also caused her worry. Marie noticed that Mary would never ring her from her home phone.

'She had started ringing me from her mobile on the way home or on the way to work. She stopped ringing me from the house. It must have been because he was there. It crossed my mind when I was talking to her.'

Incidents like these terrified Marie. She knew her suspicions were not irrational and misplaced. She slowly began to fear for her daughter Mary. No matter what she did or how she rationalised the situation; she was afraid. The two women had been more like sisters than mother and daughter. She knew that Mary was unhappy in her marriage and afraid of Whelan, but she never thought he was capable of causing her physical harm.

She last saw her only daughter and best friend alive on the afternoon of Sunday, 25 February 2001. Both Mary and Whelan had offered to drive Marie to the village of Kilmainham Wood in Co. Meath to visit Marie's 80-year-old father, Joe White, who was staying in a nursing home.

When they all met up, Marie noticed that Whelan's attitude towards his wife had changed almost beyond recognition. He ignored Mary but constantly looked at young women walking along the street. She also sensed a deep sense of bitterness between the two of them.

'Colin was not chatty. There was certainly an atmosphere between them, I felt it.'

The atmosphere got worse throughout the day. When they returned to Marie's house in Stamullen that night, she asked Mary to stay and have a cup of tea.

'She looked at him and said, "Ah no, we'll go home." And he marched out and left poor Mary to walk behind him. That's the last time I saw her. I looked out the window and all I could see was her back.'

Marie believes that Whelan had warned her not to enter her family home. She figured that her daughter had obeyed his wishes for the sake of peace and not wanting to embarrass herself by giving Whelan the opportunity to raise his voice or cause a scene.

On the following Wednesday evening, Marie rang her daughter in Balbriggan for a chat before she went to visit her father in Kilmainham Wood. Mary seemed in good form and told her that Whelan was in the gym. There was nothing unusual about the conversation and Mary seemed relaxed. She certainly wasn't worried. That conversation is etched in Marie's mind. She recalls each word spoken as if it happened yesterday.

'Mary said; which were her last words to me, "Ring me when you get home."

'I never did get a chance to ring Mary back,' recalled her mother. 'That's something I'll remember for a long time to come.'

CHAPTER 3

Within hours of having that fateful conversation, Mary was in the final throes of death. The paramedics worked frantically on her as she lay at the bottom of the stairs. They did everything in their power to save her life. But it was no use. When they applied a defibrillator to her heart it showed no reading. Mary had flatlined which meant she was clinically dead.

It was applied again and the same result appeared. But the ambulance crew hoped that she could be saved if she was rushed to hospital where doctors could restart her heart. As the paramedics tried desperately to revive her, Whelan continued acting out the role of the loving husband distraught at her worsening condition.

He pretended to cry and sobbed openly. The killer had rehearsed what he would say hundreds of times but his plan began to fall apart almost immediately.

Initially, he had wanted to keep the story straight so he wouldn't contradict himself, but in the heat of the moment he made several errors.

The first and most serious of these was when he changed the details of the story. When he was asked what had happened, he said that he was downstairs and had heard a thump. Continuing the story, he said he had found Mary at the bottom of the stairs. He went further, commenting on her ripped sleeve. Trying to make his story sound plausible, he said she must have caught herself on the bannister as she fell. But within the space of an hour, he gave a slightly different story, saying that Mary had gone to get the cat and fell down the stairs.

The truth was that no one believed a word he said; his body language was all wrong. Everyone noticed it.

When Mary was lifted onto the stretcher, Whelan stood in the hallway silent and motionless.

Privately, he feared that she was going to survive. He tried to reassure himself by asking what the paramedics interpreted as unusual questions for a grief-stricken man in his position. As they left for the hospital, Whelan hovered about asking, 'Is she dead?' as he followed the stretcher outside. The ambulance crew had never encountered such behaviour.

One paramedic answered him politely and said that it didn't look good. On hearing this, Whelan turned and walked back towards the house, but then suddenly stopped, turned on his heel, raised his voice and asked the same question again. This time he said, 'Well, is she dead or not dead?'

Again the paramedic repeated that he wasn't in a position to say.

The response Whelan gave was spine chilling.

'Ah well, I can read between the fucking lines.'

His remark took the paramedics by complete surprise. Whelan was still dressed in his dressing gown and maroon boxer shorts. On hearing the prognosis, Whelan walked into his house and changed into a pair of jeans and shirt. On the way out of the house, he swung his foot at the pet cat, Muffin, who was in the hallway.

'Get out of the way, fucking cat!' he spat at Mary's pet.

He didn't act like a man about to lose his wife. He acted like a man who could be charged with murder.

Members of Mary's family were alerted around this time. Her brother Peter was woken by voices at the front door. The caller was a fireman, accompanied by Colin's brother-in-law, who told him what had happened. They told him to go and get dressed quickly. Whelan was sitting in the waiting car.

Peter got dressed at once and got into the car. Whelan told him that Mary had fallen down the stairs at midnight. Whelan never said another word. He sat with his hand to his face crying, his head bowed.

~ ~ ~

The Accident and Emergency Department at Beaumont Hospital was notified at 12.45am that a 27-year-old woman had fallen down the stairs in her Balbriggan home. The communication stated that she was in cardiac arrest and was on her way by ambulance. This ensured that a medical team was on stand-by to commence resuscitation once she arrived. The ambulance that carried Mary travelled from Balbriggan down the M1 motorway and arrived at the hospital within 15 minutes.

When she arrived, the doctors noticed that Mary's face was cyanosed, or blue in colour. Her body also felt cold to touch. She was already dead and her face was covered in blood.

The medical staff lifted her onto a trolley where they cut her pyjama top off to get access to her veins. They also cut the bottoms off to gain access to a vein in her left leg.

The doctors on the resuscitation team established quickly that Mary was not breathing and had no cardiac output. To establish a clean airway, an anaesthetist opened Mary's mouth but noticed that her tongue was swollen and appeared larger in size.

While inserting a tube into her throat to secure and maintain an airway, the anaesthetist also noticed that the tissue around the inlet of her larynx was swollen. He put this to the back of his mind as he started ventilating Mary. He had no time to think. Time was of the essence.

But as he did so, he noticed some other marks on her neck and front of her chest which, in his view, were not consistent with just a fall down the stairs. He mentioned his concerns to the other members of the resuscitation team.

Mary next had ECG leads attached to her chest which showed a flat line; effectively there was no electrical output from her heart.

As the team did everything in their power to revive Mary, they made various attempts to find a vein to insert a drip. Eventually two veins were found, one on the leg and the other on the arm. At this point, the doctors administered a cocktail of adrenaline and atropine to aid resuscitation but Mary didn't respond to these. Nor did she respond to the physical attempts of CPR which were being carried out continuously.

Mary had been strangled. She continued to display a flat line on the monitor throughout the emergency procedure. External cardiac pacing pads were then attached to her chest and an attempt to externally pace her was made, up to the maximum available current.

But her heart and the monitor showed no response. External pacing is usually the treatment of last resort in cases of flat line cardiac arrest. It involves passing a current from the outside of the chest through the heart in an attempt to restart the heart. But this failed. She was dead. Everyone noticed that her face was dusky, a colour of light bluey-grey that would normally be associated with a person who has been dead for a while.

The doctor who led the crash team that fateful night in Beaumont Hospital was Dr Diarmuid Manning. He and his team tried to revive Mary for about 25 minutes but in the end they had to stop.

At 1.25am, having tried everything humanly possible, Dr Manning pronounced Mary dead and he recorded the time of death. His team had battled to save her life to no avail. At that moment, Whelan became a murderer.

~ ~ ~

Having gone through the formal procedure of pronouncing death, Dr Manning walked out of the resuscitation room and into the reception area where he met Whelan. He informed him that Mary had died.

At that stage, the medical team were as shocked as anyone at the death because Mary was so young, and people do not generally die from falling down the stairs. Trying to find an explanation, the doctor asked Whelan about Mary. He asked if her eyes were open and if she was moving when he found her at the bottom of the stairs. Mary was a young woman. If she had died after falling down the stairs, it was a very unusual death.

Whelan remained calm and told him that her eyes were closed and there was no movement except, he said, 'her kind of trying to breathe.' Whelan went further by telling Dr Manning that his wife had stopped breathing before the ambulance had even arrived.

In accordance with standard procedure, the doctor informed Whelan that a post-mortem would be carried out. Whelan had managed to act out the part of a worried husband but he was unable to fake grief. When he was told about the post-mortem, he did not react emotionally. He simply held his head in his hands.

His body language was all wrong and he couldn't hide this no matter how hard he tried.

When he was asked by a nurse if he would like a priest for his wife, he replied 'not at the moment.' The response struck everyone present as odd.

What he didn't know was that the deadly game was already over. Even before Mary had been formally pronounced dead, the gardaí had been alerted to the death by the night sister in Beaumont Hospital.

Catherine Galvin was an experienced medic who worked as a night sister in the casualty department of the hospital. It was this eagle-eyed nurse who first noticed that something wasn't quite right with the apparently distraught Colin Whelan.

When Mary was first admitted to Beaumont, Galvin introduced herself to Whelan. Galvin brought him into a small office where she asked him what had happened. The medics suspected that Mary's fall might have occurred as a result of some other medical condition, possibly internal. She wanted to know exactly what had happened.

Whelan repeated his fictitious story. He told Galvin that he had been watching television when he heard this thumping sound down the stairs and ran out.

Whelan gestured with his hands as he described what happened next. He said he hadn't known what to do but rang 999. He spoke about her ripped pyjama sleeve and how it had been caught on the old fashioned staircase.

Whelan began to cry at this point prompting Galvin to get some tissues for him. But as she leaned across him to get these, she noticed a scratch on the centre of his chest. As she noticed this, Whelan leaned forward even more while pretending to cry and placed his head in his hands causing his shirt to gape open. This revealed a number of large scratches on his chest. And they looked fresh.

Galvin didn't need anyone to tell her that something sinister had happened to Mary.

The night sister pretended not to notice the marks and made her excuses to leave the room. Once alone, she rang the gardaí in Balbriggan and informed them of the incident and that she had noticed scrapes on Whelan's chest.

She then went back to the resuscitation room where she was told that Mary had died.

Galvin was perturbed. She knew instinctively that something evil had happened to the dead woman. She next went out to speak with the ambulance crew who handed her a four stone engagement ring which was found on the floor of the ambulance.

She returned to the resuscitation room to check if Mary had any rings on her and found that she had no rings on her fingers at all.

She walked out to Whelan and asked him if Mary had any rings on. Whelan said his wife had two rings—an engagement ring and a wedding ring.

He seemed confused at her line of questioning. He had more pressing issues on his mind. He was preparing himself for the arrival of the gardaí.

~ ~ ~

Marie Gough was at home when she got a phone call to say that Mary had been hurt in an accident.

'When I heard that, I thought she must be hurt very bad.'

She got out of bed and woke her sons, and the family drove at speed to Beaumont Hospital. On arrival at the hospital, she made her way to the small room where Whelan was sitting with his face buried in his hands. She asked about Mary, prompting Whelan to raise his head. Without moving, he said coldly, 'She's dead.' He made no attempt to embrace her, or offer his sympathy. He just sat there. When Marie heard the news, she couldn't comprehend what had happened.

She remembers that moment vividly.

'I'll never forget the cold glare in his eyes. He was not crying. He had no emotion. He put his head down again. He made no effort to embrace me; I put my arms around him and it was like putting your arms around a stone pillar,' Marie said.

A nurse then came into the room and brought her to see her only daughter and best friend in the resuscitation room.

'It was all like a dream. I was taken down to the room where she was. The sheet was up to her chin, I remember the nurse pulled back the sheet and Mary had her pyjamas on. I remember looking at Mary's hands. Mary had long fingers. Her rings were not on her, the nurse said they probably slipped off her hands.

'Then I was looking at Mary's neck—one side was all marked and I thought, "God, she broke her neck." And I said to that nurse, "Did she suffer?" and she said, "No, she just would have gone off."

'The nurse let me stay there and I rubbed her hands and her little face.'

When she left her daughter's body, she looked directly at Whelan. She knew instinctively that he had something to do with her death; he was so emotionless. She later recalled, 'There was still no emotion from him but sure if he didn't love her, how could he grieve for her?'

~ ~ ~

In the meantime, Galvin told Whelan that his wife had arrived with no rings on. She then explained that a ring had been found on the floor of the ambulance but that Mary's wedding ring was missing. Whelan wasn't sure where all this was leading to.

But the conversation was interrupted by the arrival of the gardaí in the reception area of the hospital. Galvin left Whelan alone and met an officer named Jim O'Byrne, who she escorted to the resuscitation room where Mary's body was laid out. In the privacy of the resuscitation room, she informed him of the scrape marks she had seen on Whelan's chest. Though they dared not say it, everyone began treating the death as a murder investigation.

A short time later, Superintendent Thomas Gallagher arrived. The two officers listened carefully to what Galvin had to say before approaching Whelan. From what they could glean, nothing that Whelan said made sense.

Leaving the two gardaí alone in the relatives' room, Galvin returned to Whelan to say the gardaí wished to speak to him privately. He agreed and everyone in the relatives' room was asked to leave.

On entering the room, Gallagher began to size up Whelan. He first sympathised with him, before asking him about what had happened earlier. The account Whelan gave was similar to the one he had given earlier to the paramedics and repeated to Galvin. Once again, he said Mary had fallen down the stairs.

Gallagher was an experienced officer. He sensed that something was wrong but continued to ask very pertinent questions in an informal manner. He wanted Whelan to outline the night's events without affording him the opportunity to get his story straight.

The garda asked simple questions. He then asked Whelan if he and Mary had exchanged harsh words. Whelan immediately said 'no.'

Gallagher didn't believe him; his gut instinct told him that he was dealing with a murderer.

Experience had taught Gallagher to keep his cards close to his chest at such times. He never once allowed Whelan to suspect that he was now being treated as a murder suspect. Instead, the garda explained his actions as simply procedural which relaxed Whelan somewhat. The officer wanted Whelan to say as much as possible. In truth, everything he said was being noted as potential evidence.

After sympathising some more, Gallagher asked Whelan if he would identify Mary's dead body.

Whelan was reluctant at first to see her but then agreed to the identification. He entered the resuscitation room accompanied by Gallagher, O'Byrne and Galvin. On entering the room, he didn't get upset or attempt to hold his wife's body as is usual in such cases. Although people react to death in different ways, they all realised that there was something about Whelan's body language that was not right. Everyone present noticed it.

Moving outside the curtain, Gallagher continued to talk to and monitor Whelan, all the time explaining that he had to ask specific questions.

The killer had no reason not to trust him. At that point, Whelan had no reason to believe he was under suspicion. He fooled himself into believing he was fooling everyone. That was until Gallagher asked about the scratches on his chest.

Whelan turned visibly white when asked the question, but quickly regained his composure. He hadn't realised that he had been injured, or that Mary had scratched him.

Not knowing what to do, he looked down and pulled back his shirt to reveal even more scratch marks to his chest. When he saw the extent of his wounds, he lost his concentration momentarily.

The only thing he could think of saying was that he didn't know he was injured. Galvin pointed out four big nail scratches on his chest. When asked by Galvin if he had seen the scratches, he replied that he hadn't.

Whelan, though, possessed a remarkable ability to gather his thoughts. Knowing that he urgently needed to regain some ground, he proffered a reasonable explanation.

After a second or two, he said that Mary had grasped out at him while she was trying to catch her breath but that he did not remember being scratched.

Trying to convince the gardaí of his sincerity by being more open than required, he opened his shirt to reveal four definite marks on his chest.

Realising his mistake, he wet his fingers and rubbed his chest saying something to the effect that, 'It must be blood; there was a lot of blood.'

But no matter how hard he rubbed, the marks didn't brush away, prompting Gallagher to say they were definitive scrapes. At this point, Whelan knew he was in trouble. He had not foreseen this. He began to look panicked and worried.

It was clear to everyone in the room that he was lying through his teeth. If anything, his body language continued to give him away. All he could think of saying was, 'she was flaying around a bit with her hands when I was trying to help her.'

Gallagher remained silent for a moment before saying that it was fair enough. Not sure where he stood or whether to believe him, Whelan said he understood the situation. He then stood up and went back to his family and the Goughs.

Without hesitation, Gallagher asked Galvin if she could locate a doctor to examine Whelan and the scratch marks on his chest.

The senior garda knew he had to act fast. He knew for certain that he was dealing with a possible murder. It was crucial that he obtain a medical examination of Whelan. This could yield valuable evidence.

Just after 4am, Whelan was taken into an examination room with another officer who had arrived at the scene. This was Detective Garda Peter McCoy. He accompanied Whelan into a room where he was examined by Dr Barry Unadiae.

The doctor began by asking him how he got the scratch marks. Whelan said he did not realise he had them until Galvin pointed them out. Dr Unadiae next asked if he had been involved in an assault or fight over the last few days to which Whelan said he wasn't.

The doctor then asked Whelan to take his shirt off. This revealed even more wounds and scratch marks, much to Whelan's horror.

The doctor observed a number of marks on the left of his chest just above the breast. These three marks extended across and towards the midline of the chest. The centre scratch of these three was more prominent.

But the doctor also noticed two superficial marks on the right side of his chest. There were also two more superficial marks on the right shoulder. And there were three more marks just above the left lower rib. These injuries were consistent with a fight but there was no bruising or swelling on Whelan's body. This suggested that his attacker was of a lighter build.

When the examination was completed, Whelan left the room accompanied by Galvin and waited for Detective McCoy. As they waited, Whelan told the nurse that he worked as a computer analyst and was self-employed. He acted out the part of a heartbroken husband.

He said he wished he could turn the clock back just one hour, and then he went on to mention that he had fallen down the stairs himself previously, and that everyone knew this.

Galvin reassured him saying that he had done his best for Mary. Given that she certainly feared she was in the company of an evil killer, Galvin remained remarkably calm. She chatted to Whelan without arousing any suspicion. But the conversation inevitably returned to the subject of what had happened.

Whelan introduced another element to his fictitious story when he said that Mary had just showered. At this point, he appeared to be thinking methodically about his story. During this conversation, he mentioned that he didn't think Mary had washed her hair.

It had occurred to the medical staff that Mary's hair was very dry for someone who had just showered. There was also no smell of perfume, deodorant or talcum powder from her body. What appeared to be an irrelevant detail was, in fact, crucial because it showed that Whelan was lying over the small details.

After a short time, O'Byrne and Galvin returned to the resuscitation room and removed a neck chain and a gold bracelet from Mary's body.

Galvin handed these items and the engagement ring to O'Byrne. While removing the neck chain, Galvin noticed what looked like a ligature mark on Mary's neck. It was located in a centre position on the neck and was somewhere between two and three inches in length. The towel Whelan had carefully wrapped around his wife's neck to disguise the strangulation had left a tell tale sign.

Galvin personally needed no convincing. She told the gardaí exactly what Whelan had told her and highlighted the inconsistencies in his story. She said she had asked him if Mary was conscious or moving when he first found her at the bottom of the stairs. Whelan had initially answered, 'no, she was just taking shallow breaths.' Therefore she could not have inflicted the scratch marks apparent on his chest. She also pointed out that when Mary was first brought into the resuscitation room, she was very cold. In fact, Galvin said she asked the ambulance crew how long had she been in cardiac arrest. The gardaí needed no convincing. They knew it was murder.

CHAPTER 4

Despite all his planning and research into how to commit the perfect crime, Colin Whelan missed the basics. When Mary was rushed to hospital, the gardaí had been called to 49 Clonard Street. He hadn't seen the arriving patrol car and therefore didn't know that one of the fire officers who arrived at the scene told the gardaí that Mary was unlikely to make it.

Although Whelan had left his house locked and secure, the gardaí decided to remain at the scene, should the case become a murder investigation. Once he left the house for the hospital, Whelan effectively abandoned the scene of his crime and the forensics that he had left behind. This was another serious mistake. What he never envisaged was that Mary's body itself would reveal a catalogue of damning evidence. Her body was removed from Beaumont Hospital at 9.55am the following morning and transferred to the city morgue on the Malahide Road.

Uniformed gardaí remained with the body until the State Pathologist Dr Marie Cassidy arrived an hour later to carry out her post-mortem.

It was at this point that Whelan began to lose control. Events overtook him. Before he left Beaumont, one of the gardaí asked him to call into Balbriggan Garda Station and make a statement about the previous night's events. Whelan was told that this was procedural and that he had nothing to worry about.

On arrival at the station, he was treated with courtesy and taken into an interview room by Detective Garda Peter McCoy. Superintendent Gallagher also sat in, believing it crucial to get him on the record before he had time to gather his thoughts and work out a more thorough alibi. He repeated his fabricated story to the two gardaí.

The following is a memo of the statement he made.

'I hereby declare that this statement is true to the best of my knowledge and belief and that I make it knowing that if it is tendered in evidence I will be liable to prosecution if I state in it anything which I know to be false or do not believe to be true.

'I resided with my wife Mary at 49 Clonard Street, Balbriggan, Co. Dublin. We are living at this address since August 1997. We got married on 09/09/00. I knew Mary about nine years and have been going out with her for about seven years. We got engaged on 09/10/1998. Mary was a Gough from Cockhill, Stamullen, Co. Meath. I am originally from Gormanstown, Co. Meath. My mother and father are residing there. I have two sisters and one brother.

'I work as a computer analyst with Irish Permanent in Stephens Green, Dublin. I am on contract with them. I have worked at the same job for the last nine years. I travel by train to work every day from Balbriggan. Mary worked as a legal secretary with Declan Wade Solicitors, Swords. She travelled by car to work every day. The house at 49 Clonard Street was in the family for years and I purchased it four years ago. We have no family together.

'Yesterday, 28th February 2001 both of us left for work at the usual times, i.e. at around 8am. Mary leaves at about 8.15am. I rang Mary in Declan Wade's office about twice during the day. I arrived home at about 6pm. Mary was in ahead of me. Mary started to get the dinner ready and I went to the gym in Balbriggan. I left at about 6.30pm and arrived back at about 7.30pm. Mary complained of having a migraine headache. She thought it was that she was so hungry as both of us had started a Detox programme on Ash Wednesday morning. I had my dinner when I came back from the gym. Mary had already eaten.

'My sister Clodagh Brassil telephoned at around 8pm to see how we were getting on on the Detox programme. We both watched telly for a while and I loaded the dishwasher. I drove Mary to the Detox programme at Drogheda, Co. Louth. We arrived at his house just shortly after nine. I think his name is Michael Hughes. We came straight back, arriving at home at about 9.45pm. We sat down and compared reports from the Detox programme for about 15 minutes.

'I then went upstairs and shaved and showered. I then came down to Mary in the sitting room at about 10.30pm or 10.40pm. I was dressed in my bathroom robe. We sat for about a half an hour. Mary then went upstairs to have a shower at about 11.15pm. We have a cat which sleeps at the bottom of the stairs in a bed which is attached to the radiator. Mary was around upstairs for a good while.

'At about 12 midnight, I heard a series of thuds and I knew straight away that Mary had fallen down the stairs. There is carpet on the stairs. I went straight out to the stairs and saw Mary was at the bottom of the stairs in the hall. Her head was pointing towards the front door with one leg on the stairs. She was more on her back than on her side. Mary was moaning and she tried to move her upper part of her body. I knelt down beside her and saw blood coming from her nose; her eyes were open. She clutched me with her right hand. I cannot remember where she grabbed me. She was more on her left hand side. I ran upstairs and got a bathroom towel. I think it was a yellow one. She was frothing on the nose and bleeding heavy.

'I panicked and after a few minutes I rang 999 on the house phone, which is in the sitting room. I gave directions to the ambulance control. He was giving me medical advice and instructed me how to give mouth to mouth resuscitation. I blew into her mouth a number of times. I was instructed to keep her warm and got a duvet from upstairs. The Balbriggan Fire Brigade arrived after a short time and moved Mary into the computer room. The ambulance arrived a short time later.

'I travelled to Beaumont Hospital with my brother in

law, Jimmy Brassil. I have no recollection of any breathing from Mary after I came down with the towel. The left sleeve in Mary's pyjamas was torn when she was lying at the bottom of the stairs. I have marks on my chest which I think Mary done to me when she grabbed me as she struggled. I did not get them anywhere else. I had a good relationship with Mary and we did not have any dispute last night. I was wearing a navy dressing gown with a white stripe. I have heard this statement read over and it is correct.

Signed: Colin Whelan

Securing a signed statement from Whelan was a major coup for the infant investigation. The two gardaí once again sympathised with Whelan before sending him on his way.

~ ~ ~

The Gough's left the hospital at around 5am, shortly after Whelan. Marie, accompanied by her family, drove to Whelan's parental home in Gormanstown to await his return from Balbriggan Garda Station. Marie wanted to speak to him. She knew the gardaí had taken his house keys, so he had nowhere else to stay. More than anything she wanted to know exactly what had happened.

Mary was much loved by Whelan's family and his own parents were devastated by the news and were openly distressed when Marie arrived at their home. They invited her into the house to comfort her. After a while, Whelan arrived but when he walked into the room he ignored her.

'I knew by the face of him. I knew straight away by the way he looked at me that he didn't want me there. He didn't come over and hug me. So after a while, we got up and left.'

Marie still couldn't bring herself to believe that Whelan could have been responsible. She figured that he simply didn't like her and was too traumatised to know right from wrong at that particular time.

~ ~ ~

Back at the city morgue, Dr Marie Cassidy had begun her post-mortem. Within hours of the murder, she confirmed the suspicions that Mary had not simply fallen down the stairs; she had been murdered. Examining Mary carefully, she began a painstaking examination of the body. She searched for clues as to what happened. The first thing she noticed was that Mary's face was markedly congested and cyanosed, or purple in colour. She also found pinpoint haemorrhages over the eyelids and blotchy haemorrhages on the inside of the right lower eyelid. These were also present in the temple areas, in front of the ears and also behind the left ear. She also found pinpoint haemorrhages on the inside of the mouth.

She dictated her findings as she worked through the examination. Importantly, she noted superficial scratch marks over the front of the right upper thigh, running down and outwards. On the front of the upper left thigh there were some haphazardly arranged, very superficial, scratch marks.

Dr Cassidy noted that she had been informed that this lady was admitted to Beaumont Hospital having been said to have fallen down stairs. However the post-mortem examination showed that Mary had died from asphyxia due to strangulation.

Dr Cassidy found an incomplete ligature mark on the right side of Mary's neck as well as other marks on the surface of the neck. More to the point, there was evidence of gross asphyxial signs above the ligature mark; these were the tell tale signs of strangulation.

There was also damage to the tongue which happens in the course of strangulation.

The pathologist also noted bruising of the deep neck tissues but no damage to the larynx itself. For the benefit of the garda investigation, she said this was not uncommon in a young person as the larynx is made of cartilage which is pliable; it can withstand a fair degree of force before it would be broken.

More importantly, Dr Cassidy failed to find any other serious wounds. She found very few minor marks or injuries to the body which one would expect in a serious fall. Although she found some bruising on Mary's arms, she said these were probably caused by gripping.

In plain English, Mary's injuries were not consistent with a fall. And they certainly wouldn't have caused her death.

Death due to a fall down a stairs is normally associated with a significant head injury, a fracture of the cervical spine or the bones of the neck, none of which was present in this case. She concluded that the cause of death was asphyxia and compression of the neck, or strangulation with the use of a ligature.

News of the post-mortem was communicated to Gallagher that afternoon. This put Whelan in the frame as the prime suspect but the gardaí decided to wait a full day before informing him about the cause of death. They wanted to do their homework.

~ ~ ~

Later that same afternoon, Whelan came over to Marie's family home. The house was full of people. When he entered the house, he walked straight to Marie and embraced her. She knew instinctively that it was just for show. Whelan acted out the part of a grief-stricken husband but all the time was watching those around him.

Any suspicions Marie secretly harboured about Whelan were confirmed that night when two detectives arrived at her front door. They wanted to speak to her privately. When she was introduced to them, she noticed they were agitated.

'They asked me, did I think this or did I think that, had I any suspicions. I said to myself, "What are they talking about?"

'I now know they were only trying to prepare me for what I was going to hear the next day.'

After the detectives left, Marie and some of her family went over to Whelan's home. The house was also full to capacity with sympathisers.

Whelan sat with a number of his friends in one room while his family sat in another room. He knew he was under suspicion although no one had said anything to him. Marie was accompanied by her son.

'I remember I went up to see Colin and he wasn't anxious to see me at all. He was sitting on the bed and was busy on the mobile phone.

'Colin hardly acknowledged me; he was not interested in my presence. Colin was saying it was a conspiracy by the gardaí. Colin was in no way mourning. I could not take this in, I had lost my daughter. Colin showed no interest in me, he never even asked me how I was.'

That her son-in-law ignored her didn't upset Marie to the extent that one would expect. She held her nerve and chose to rise above his behaviour. The truth was that Whelan was starting to panic. He had begun to talk about hiring a solicitor.

Mary's brother, Séamus, would later tell the gardaí that he heard Whelan say as much when he visited his family home that evening.

'Colin was mentioning to his brother-in-law about getting a solicitor. Colin was very alert and in no way seemed upset. This surprised me. Anyway, at the time we all felt sympathy for Colin.'

~ ~ ~

The next day on Friday afternoon, the Gough family were told Mary had been strangled to death. Marie was not shocked; she was devastated. There was nothing she could say or do. She accepted their word and thanked the detectives for their help.

Whelan heard the news that his farcical charade had been exposed at the same time when Gallagher, accompanied by Detective Superintendent John McElligot, visited Whelan at his parents' house.

On arrival at the house, they decided not to disclose the precise outcome of the post-mortem examination. Instead they would tell him part of the story and gauge his response. The two investigators were polite when they entered the house and spoke to Whelan in an amicable manner. But they made no bones about the purpose of their visit. They told Whelan the results of the post-mortem totally contradicted his version of events.

He went as white as a ghost and simply said this couldn't be true and that it was an outrageous thing to say. They left it at that.

Marie's son, Séamus, visited the Whelan home that evening to gauge for himself what was happening. When he arrived at the house, he went up to talk to Whelan in his bedroom.

'When I opened the door, Colin was sitting facing us with his feet up on a puff. I cannot remember how the conversation started but Colin said the only emotion he felt was anger.

'He said, "She fell down the stairs; if they think I done it why am I sitting here?" He said every car he heard he thought it was the detectives. I know Colin asked about the body being released; when was this going to happen?

'He said, "I suppose your mother will get the body for funeral arrangements."'

Séamus was struck by the way Whelan referred to his dead sister. In all that conversation, he referred to Mary as 'the body' which Séamus found unbearable. But he was more worried about Whelan's topic of conversation. He was obsessed by the gardaí.

While he was in the house, he heard Whelan say aloud, 'If they think I did do it, why aren't they arresting me? They're up in the trees watching me.'

Minutes later, Whelan said, 'I wish I was not there when she fell down the stairs. I wish I had been down the town or something else; that I came back and found her.'

Drawing more attention to himself, he even started talking about strangulation. Séamus overheard him say, 'What do they mean strangulation, was it with a piece of clothing, manual strangulation or asphyxiation?'

Séamus stood his ground and was not intimidated by Whelan, although he was confused. He couldn't bring himself to believe that his brother-in-law was a killer.

All he could think of saying was, 'What can I say?'

Whelan then launched into his alibi saying, 'I was in the house with Mary, there was only the two of us, I was in the sitting-room watching TV. I heard thud, thud, thud and when I opened the door I found her at the bottom of the stairs.'

Séamus stayed for ten minutes at the house before leaving. Whelan never said goodbye and never spoke to him again.

~ ~ ~

The following day, shortly after 5pm, Gallagher and a detective named Michael Considine returned to the Whelan residence. They were shown into the sitting-room where Whelan, his parents and a number of other people were assembled. Gallagher asked if they could speak with him alone. Whelan was afraid and desperately trying to rally support. He refused to talk to them alone and said that he wanted his family present. Gallagher then informed Colin that the findings of the post-mortem examination showed conclusively that Mary had been strangled and the gardaí were now investigating a murder.

He looked at Whelan directly and informed him that in the event of him wishing to make any comment he would have to caution him. He then cautioned him further saying, 'You are not obliged to say anything unless you wish to do so but anything you may say will be taken down in writing and may be given in evidence.'

Whelan replied, 'It's not possible, it's not possible,' at the same time striking the arm of the chair with his hand. He was not under arrest but the gardaí wanted him to know that he had fooled no one. They wanted him to know that everyone knew he was a killer.

~ ~ ~

In the midst of this terrible nightmare, Marie showed herself to be courageous. Later that same day, she called a family meeting, gathering everyone to the family home.

'I didn't want them to read about Mary's death in the papers or hear it on the radio. I called them all together and I told them what happened. Everyone was very, very upset. You could say they were stunned.'

She told the family to leave the detective work to the gardaí and that they should prepare to bury Mary. Everyone knew Whelan was the killer but he was now irrelevant. What mattered now was Mary.

Fearing his imminent arrest, Whelan decided to try to mend his relationship with his in-laws. He saw their support as crucial if he was to be charged with murder. He was now paranoid and terrified.

~ ~ ~

That weekend, Mary's brother Peter received an unexpected phone call from one of Colin's friends. He said Colin wanted him to call over. Peter wasn't afraid of Colin and arrived over that Saturday.

Whelan was waiting in the sitting-room. On entering the room, Peter sat on the chair beside him. He opened the conversation.

'Hello, how are you doing?'

Whelan came straight to the point.

'I don't know what's happening. I don't know where they are getting these stories from. I think they are trying to split the families up. I know Mary seven years and in that time I never did or never would hurt her.'

Peter listened and never said a word as Whelan protested his innocence.

'The gardaí have not come near the house, they have not arrested me or hauled me in. I don't know what's going on.

'Did you not get the same story as we did? Were the gardaí not with you? As far as I am concerned the gardaí have split the families up.'

There was silence.

'I am not thick or stupid. I know that the funeral is going to be handed over to your mother but I want to be there.'

Peter later told the gardaí that he then asked Whelan what had happened that night. Whelan repeated his lie and rambled on about how he had been watching television when he heard a crash.

Peter then asked him out straight if he was alone in the house.

'Are you sure there was no one else in the house; maybe someone came in without you knowing?'

'No, no, I was the only one in the house.'

Whelan thought he had scored a home run. He actually convinced himself that Peter believed him. When he had finished lying, he thanked the grieving brother for calling by but was struck when Peter said nothing more.

CHAPTER 5

The gardaí had stayed away from Whelan for operational reasons; they didn't want him to know they had amassed a wealth of information on him. Gallagher, and the others leading the murder hunt, ordered that he be kept in the dark about everything.

He was their only suspect; there was no one else in the frame.

In a murder investigation, the senior officers in charge try to gather as much evidence and information on their suspect as is humanly possibly. From the start, Gallagher had acted with speed and co-ordination in preserving evidence and taking notes of everything Whelan had said. Every scrap of information on their target was analysed. The team didn't leave anything to chance.

Given the nature of the murder, and the fact that Whelan had used a ligature to strangle his wife, Gallagher rightly suspected that Whelan had read up on murder, and probably had planned the killing. Knowing that Whelan worked with computers and software, the gardaí sought a search warrant to seize his office machine and work records. They wanted everything. The detectives wanted to know who he emailed, what websites he viewed and what he did in his spare time. Such clandestine intelligence gathering would give them an insight into the real Colin Whelan.

To this end, Gallagher attended Dublin District Court on the morning of Saturday, 3 March and obtained a search warrant to enter the Irish Permanent Building Society on St Stephens Green, and seize relevant material.

As far as the enquiry team was concerned, there was no doubt that Whelan was their man. From day one, there had been no other suspect and all lines of investigation ran straight back to him. But to convict him of murder, they needed solid evidence. They also had to establish a reasonable motive.

They hoped that Whelan's computer would contain some clue that could help solve the crime. But as they removed the computer from the Irish Permanent office on St Stephen's Green, not even the most optimistic detective on the team could have imagined what it would reveal.

With his extensive knowledge of computers, Whelan should have known that deleting the internet history files on his own terminal wasn't enough to cover his tracks. A large company like Irish Permanent has hundreds of terminals feeding into a central server which automatically retains details of each person's internet use.

As part of the enquiry, Gallagher had sought specialist assistance from the Computer Department at the Garda Bureau of Fraud Investigation. When Whelan's terminal was handed over for examination, the computer specialists uncovered a virtual goldmine of information. But the evidence retrieved from the computer's hard drive was not the normal type of information found by gardaí.

The evidence revealed that Whelan was no ordinary killer; he was a dark and sinister man, fascinated by strangulation and sex.

Many of the gardaí on the case had never encountered a criminal like him; few men of his calibre had ever been brought to justice.

His computer showed that he had a deep interest in strangulation and asphyxiation.

The computer analysts downloaded information on all internet searches that Whelan conducted in the months leading up to Mary's death. When detectives began to individually examine the websites he accessed, they discovered they all had a common link. The websites gave information on murder, specifically the murder of women through strangulation. What's more, analysis of his hard drive revealed that Whelan enjoyed a sinister devotion to an American serial killer called Henry Louis Wallace.

Few of the detectives assigned to bring Whelan to justice had ever dealt with anything like it.

Wallace was an incorrigible serial killer. In April 1994, he was indicted for the murders of nine women; Caroline Love, Shawna Hack, Audrey Ann Spain, Valencia Jumper, Michelle Stinson, Vanessa Little Mack, Betty Jean Baucom, Brandi June Henderson and Deborah Slaughter, over a two-year period between 1992 and 1994. Wallace was an impoverished black crack cocaine addict who was also indicted for rape, sexual assault, robbery with a dangerous weapon, and assault inflicting serious injury.

In the early days of his murderous spree, Wallace was incredibly careful. He forensically cleaned his crime scenes and made his victims look like they had died in accidents.

He also had an unusual calling card. When he took a life, he used towels and bedsheets to cover the victims' bodies. Once he was satisfied that death had occurred, he kept the victim's body warm in order to disguise the precise time of death. But there was another undeniable comparison. Wallace never strangled women with his bare hands; he used a ligature to try to disguise the tell tale signs of asphyxiation.

Wallace was finally caught when he killed three women in a lust-filled rampage lasting 48 hours. In custody, he spoke freely about his horrific crimes and told police about the women's final words and actions. He even spoke about their agony when he applied what he called the 'Boston Choke' on them to render them powerless.

On the surface, Whelan's decision to murder his wife had been treated as a case of domestic violence. When the murder team began studying

Wallace's modus operandi, they quickly realised that Whelan was a copycat killer.

Like Wallace, Whelan had used a ligature to strangle Mary. He had also tried to keep her corpse warm by covering it with a duvet.

As the detectives spent more and more time making comparisons between the two men, it became clear that Whelan had replicated Wallace's modus operandi. There was no doubt.

Some believed that Whelan was actually obsessed with Wallace, who gained a certain degree of notoriety because of the women he butchered. This is what interested Whelan the most.

Wallace's first victim was Caroline Love, who shared a flat with his girlfriend. She died after Wallace used his girlfriend's key to get into her flat, and hid in the bathroom waiting for her to come home from work. When she arrived home, he told her he wanted to make love. She resisted, prompting him to attack.

'I kept the hold on her until she passed out. And at that time I moved her to her bedroom and removed her clothes, had intercourse with her, and at the same time I was still applying the choke hold. She began to fight so I used a curling iron that was near her bed and I placed the cord around her neck.'

After she died, Wallace folded the body in her own bedsheets in a bid to keep her body warm. However, he panicked after the murder and decided to dump the body in the wilderness.

His next victim was Shawna Hawk. Wallace later told police, 'I rendered the choke hold on her until she passed out. And then I filled the bathtub with water and placed her in it.'

Audrey Spain was his third victim. He also choked her to render her helpless. She blacked out. He stripped her, dragged her to her bedroom, and raped her.

'She was coming to, and she begged me not to hurt her so I just performed sex on her, and then I told her to stand and put her clothes on. And as she stood up to put her underwear on, that's when I administered the choke hold,' he said.

Next to die was Valencia Jumper. Like Mary, she died after a towel was looped around her neck. Wallace later said, 'I put the towel around her neck and she just went out real quick. I went to her kitchen and I noticed there was a bottle of rum.

'I poured the rum all over her body and I went into the kitchen and opened a can of pork and beans and put it on the stove. I took the battery out of her smoke detector and I turned the stove on high. I went back to her bedroom and I took a match and I threw it on the rum. I left and went home.'

He next murdered Michelle Stinson.

'I went to the bathroom and I got a towel, put it around her neck and I strangled her. But she kept moaning and groaning and so forth and so on, so there was a knife in her kitchen, and I think I stabbed her about four times.'

The gardaí could see comparisons with every case. Vanessa Mack was victim number six. Wallace put a pillowcase around her neck before killing her.

Gardaí were startled by the similarity between Mary's shocking murder and the technique used by Wallace to kill his victims.

It all started to come unstuck when Wallace embarked on a two-day killing spree that started with Betty Baucom.

Like Mary, Betty fought back, inflicting scratches and a bite mark on Wallace's shoulder.

He later told police, 'I placed a towel around her neck and asked her if she had any money.' She told him she had some in her purse and gave it to him. He then strangled her.

Wallace said of the murder to police, 'We had intercourse and afterwards she got on her knees and started praying because she was scared. And I said, "I'm not going to hurt you. Give me a hug" and she hugged me, but I choked her out with a towel until she was red in the face and unconscious.'

He killed Brandi June Henderson in a similar fashion to the other victims, using sheets to keep her body warm after he ensured that she had died.

Debra Slaughter was Wallace's ninth victim. There was no logic to the murder. Wallace later said, 'I caught her arm and I grabbed the knife from her and I stabbed her about 20 times.'

In January 1997 Wallace was sentenced to death. He is currently on death row in North Carolina.

The gardaí now knew Whelan was far more dangerous and cunning than anyone had previously imagined.

When the investigators began checking the dates when he first took an interest in murder, they discovered he had spent weeks on research. He looked at the methods used by other killers—some of whom had struck in the last century.

One murder he had a gruesome interest in was the horrific murder of Carrie Brown, a prostitute murdered in New York in 1891. It has always been suggested that she was killed by Jack the Ripper on a visit to New York.

The cause of her death was strangulation by a portion of clothing tied around the throat, and incisions to the lower abdomen, intestines, and vagina.

The gardaí found Whelan's fascination with death perturbing. He had also studied the murder of Julie Ybanez in Missouri in 1999. She was strangled by her 17-year-old son Nathan, who was later convicted of first degree murder.

Another American murderer Whelan studied was David Magraw, who strangled his wife Nancy in 1990 on the same day they were set to meet with divorce lawyers to discuss a settlement.

Magraw had expressed anger when his wife refused to accept his offer of $10,000, yet Magraw's assets were estimated at $800,000. Magraw also interested Whelan because the killer had been having an affair with a 22-year-old woman. Strangulation using a ligature was the common denominator in all the cases.

Whelan's reading list resembled a who's who of psycho killers. But he always returned to the case of the State v Wallace from the Supreme Court of North Carolina. Whelan was fixated on Wallace.

When the Fraud Squad ran further checks on the hard drive, they discovered that Whelan had even downloaded the pages of his court trial.

Whelan replicated Wallace's murderous style of strangulation when he took his wife's life. But he developed and streamlined it.

He searched for ways to asphyxiate on the internet typing in the words 'deaths involving asphyxiation' on search engines.

He familiarised himself with strangulation techniques and read as much as he could. This is text from one internet site that Whelan read before killing his wife:

'Strangulation is asphyxiation from compression on the neck. It can be done manually or with a ligature like a rope, binder, a neck tie. Strangulation may also be caused by hard blows to the neck. Judo or karate chops to the throat may cause damage to the larynx, followed by suffocation. Manual strangulation is a homicide.

'A person cannot strangle himself with his hands because when he loses consciousness his hands relax and his breathing resumes. In manual strangulation, the attackers fingernails often make small tell tale bruises or marks on the neck. But the marks on the neck will not show the direction from which the victim was attacked. Fingernails vary, too, in size and shape. Another sign of manual strangulation is hemorrhaging in the throat area, this can be seen in an autopsy. Sometimes a fracture of the hyoid bone, a U-shaped bone at the base of the tongue is also found.

'Strangulation by ligature may be homicidal or

suicidal,' the website reads. 'The ligature often is made from something handy at the scene. Pajamas, neckties, belts, electrical cords, ladies' stockings and other items can be used. Strangulation by a garrote of rope or wire sometimes is used in homicidal strangulation but it is not seen very often. Close inspection of the marks left on the skin may show the type of garrote used.'

At the time, Whelan wasn't an employee of Irish Permanent; he had his own company which supplied IT services on contract to the bank. However, he had his own work station on the fifth floor of the bank's head office on St Stephens Green. It was here that many of his sinister internet searches took place.

Once they took possession of the computer, the gardaí were able to get inside the mind of Colin Whelan. The investigation team quickly discovered that he had been planning the murder for at least seven months. A forensic trawl of the computer showed that three weeks before the couple married, Whelan had begun to search for information on how to kill Mary in earnest. In the weeks that followed, the gardaí found out that he conducted at least 22 searches for ways to murder Mary. As Mary prepared for her wedding, Whelan surfed the internet for information on 'asphyxiation' and 'smothering.'

A number of dates stood out from the others. The investigation team discovered that on 17 August, less than a month before the couple wed, Whelan began to search the internet in more depth.

The investigation team compiled times and dates for a book of evidence. One computer record showed that at 11.45am that same morning, he typed the word 'asphyxiate' into a search engine. Two minutes later, all the while keeping up the façade of doing his normal job, he widened his search, typing in 'how to asphyxiate.'

He conducted similar searches on 2 January—just weeks before he killed his wife. This time he input a different term—'smothering'. He also typed in the words 'blocking the air supply'.

While sifting through his computer records, the gardaí came to conclude that he was not a spur of the moment killer, but a psychopath. The list of internet trawls he performed shocked the enquiry team. From his computer records, he appeared to be someone completely obsessed with strangulation.

Gallagher was informed of the breakthrough. And even someone with his wealth of experience was taken aback.

On some days, Whelan could spend hours at work reading about murder and death. On one day alone—19 February—he conducted no fewer than seven online searches in a frenetic burst of activity between 12.15pm and 1pm on that particular day. Three days later, he accessed the website of the North Carolina Supreme Court where he studied the methods used by Wallace.

The gardaí were stunned at this. Few Irish criminals had ever replicated the methods of serial killers and psychopaths. Whelan was the first known to Gallagher and many others on the case.

While Whelan looked up ways to commit the perfect murder by copying infamous killers, he also found time to post personal ads for extramarital affairs, search for swingers online and look up adult websites which were of an explicit nature. From his yahoo account, he searched for extramarital fun.

In November 2000, two months after he wed, Whelan looked up the adult website, Private Affairs Introduction Service.

Whelan checked out one woman's profile which read:

'"Mary" from Trim, Co. Meath. Aged 30.' The married woman said she was 'looking for a cyber affair at first but maybe more . . .'

Whelan often searched adult websites which showed sexually explicit material. He was obsessed by sex and infidelity. He used various means to try to meet other women. Often, he would post his own details on the internet and see what happened. On 4 January 2000 at 7am, he posted the following advert seeking a pen pal.

'Hi, my name is Colin, I'm a true red blooded Irish male, 29 years young. Into music scene, good food and wine etc, like to enjoy the beauty of nature as often as possible. Hope to chat to either sex, of any age, race, religion or creed. So go on drop me a line, you may enjoy the Celtic experience.'

His ad attracted two responses. A woman called Tina from Canada replied as did an American woman named Linda.

'I am from Canada, as you say I am also a red blooded Irish woman but have lived here all my life. I am interested in learning about Ireland and all my cultural background. I would like a pen pal with intelligence and integrity. If you're interested in mature conversation, please reply, Tina.'

Whelan replied saying he liked to spend his time socialising. He said he played rugby and was in a band that played local pubs, 'just for a laugh rather than the money.'

'Well, I just finished renovating an old house, took me 2 years but it was worth it in the end, everything I have always dreamed of . . . as well as the parties that I can hold there,' he emailed.

'Outside of work myself and a couple of friends try to travel at weekends as much as possible around Ireland to the different festivals, the craic does be mighty and you never know what to expect, they are great,' he told the Canadian woman.

Linda from North Carolina told Whelan that she was married, loved Irish music especially the Three Irish Tenors. Whelan said he was going on his holidays to Bali with friends, never mentioning his wife Mary. He conducted correspondence with both women for a time but nothing came of it.

This type of conversation didn't interest Whelan. Having failed to ignite much response, he signed up to an adult website called www.iwantu.com under the username Celtic Tackle. He also surfed the net for the Swingers Ireland message board which offers swing and kinky theme parties.

He found no one willing to engage in his fantasies on the adult sites but he did receive a response from the ad he placed looking for a pen-pal. When the gardaí began reading his emails, they discovered that Whelan was heavily involved in an online romance with a Welsh woman.

CHAPTER 6

In late December 2000, he had started writing to Helen Sheppard, who was a Welsh woman in her late 30s. They initially met through internet chat rooms on www.yahoo.com. He used the pseudonyms Celtic Tackle and later Furry Bear and Mr Bear in his correspondence.

Sheppard had lived in the town of Porth in Wales for the past six years and had been married twice but both relationships had ended in divorce. She had two children from her first marriage. She was employed as an area manager with the Imperial Cancer Research Fund and had worked with the organisation for the past six years. Her job involved travelling around Wales visiting various charity shops. She worked from her living room where she operated a fax machine, a telephone and an old computer that was not connected to the internet. She met Whelan after receiving a new laptop computer with internet access. Her brother had uploaded a profile of his sister on Yahoo which included photographs and a short description of her.

Sheppard enjoyed the internet and contributed to various chatrooms. She spoke to many people on the internet but one stood out from the others. This man identified himself as Celtic Tackle.

Sheppard was interested. When she viewed his profile, it showed a photograph of a good-looking male model. This profile gave the name Colin and stated that he was 29 years of age, single and good-looking.

When she read the profile, she figured the details were possibly correct but she did not believe that the photograph was of him. She was right. Whelan had superimposed his own head onto a model's body.

She considered it all a bit of fun. She often talked to Celtic Tackle each week, sometimes for about two hours in the evening.

Childhood snaps of Mary Gough. She was only 27-years-old when she was brutally murdered by her husband, Colin Whelan.

To: Tweets

Cheers!
To your Health!

To your health, I'll have a few beers for you tonight Ok...

Yeah you're sick alright... nothing bloody wrong with your mind......

Hey Fur balls funny made me laugh, good card |o|, although you do have the time to look for them eh... better to have fur balls that birdie legs eh... only joking, I've had a quick peek at them... Hey I have a saying when a girl goes on about her legs..... I know it doesn't apply to you little chick.... Hmmm legs "I've seen a better pair of legs hanging out of a nest" it gets a clip around the ear all the time..... ahhh ouch wasn't referring to you at all Tweets...
You mean you're goin crazier (if that's a word) no way. Can't happen... been there already helen got the t-shirt crazy bird.. here open wide just another few paracetemols..... you're goin more delirious by the minute.... I'll have to water you down keep you nice and cool.... Honey eh Hmmm sticks to my fur but... can always compromise, I'll keep my paws off and just use my imagination, ah shit spilt my coffee......... see what you do to me.... Hey three times eh... you trying to be funny eh, insinutating something or trying to plant seeds in my head, hey you know the saying Three times a lady......... and more is a mmmmm....... Good friend of mine....|o| .. what d'ya mean I don't give you enough kisses, jesus, that's nice eh... any more and I'd be up for assault, well anymore in my mind anyway.... Right short and sweet I'm away.

Above: This is the last email Whelan sent his online girlfriend, just hours before he strangled his wife. He pretended to be in Germany at the time. The common demoninator in his emails, is that they all contained lies. Whelan told Helen Sheppard that his wife had died the previous year.

Mary's mother, Marie Gough, said she was the type of girl who could stand on her own two feet. She was independent. Mary was always honest and decent.
Courtesy of the Irish Daily Star on Sunday

Inset: An excited Mary on her way to a debs. Mary was a very popular young woman, who was invited to two debs balls as well as her own.

Above and left: Colin Whelan on his way from court after pleading guilty to the charge of murdering his wife.
© *Collins Photo Agency*

Opposite page: Whelan increased the insurance policy on his wife's life and then spent months on the internet researching how to murder her. He entered 'sudden loss of consciousness' and 'asphyxiation' as key words on search engines.

Below: Marie Gough and family members leave the court
© *Collins Photo Agency*

£56.31.

Colin Whelan,
49 Clonard Street,
Balbriggan,
Co. Dublin.

27/04/2000.

Louise,

I received a Life Cash Cover quote from yourself a number of weeks ago for the value of £200k for a dual life policy. I have now enclosed a completed application form for a Life Cash Cover policy for your attention. When myself and my fiancee detailed our commitments etc we felt that the initial quote value would not be sufficient, partly because I am self employed etc. I have increased the amount of Life cover to be £400k dual life on the application form. I would be obliged if you could contact me with the revised monthly repayment before proceeding with the application to ensure that I am content with same. I have detailed my work number below for contact purposes.

Yours Sincerely,

Colin Whelan -
Colin Whelan.
01-7020315.

Rang client will quote for above on 2-5-00
o client accepted prem at £56.31 a month

Martin Sweeney, who lived close to Colin Whelan, was another
innocent victim. Whelan stole Sweeneys' identity and used his passport
to escape to Spain where he lived until he was identified by an Irish
tourist and extradited back to Ireland.
Courtesy of the Irish Daily Star on Sunday

Mary Gough

Our outgoing girl with a great zest for life and her family. She loved life, family friends, and Muffin the cat. She was very much her own person.

Marie Gough, Margaret McNulty, James Gough, your friends and family miss you every day.

To Mary
Thanks for all the happy times, laughs and the very proud moments. We'll walk together through life until we meet again

Love always and forever, brother Dave and Ashly

Miss you always Mary, think of you all the time - Love Nicola
I miss you more than words can say, my life long friend - Sinead

Mary you were...
Our friend, Our companion
Through good times and bad
Our buddy
Through happy and sad,
Beside us you stood, beside us you walked
You were there to listen, you were there to talk
With happiness, with smiles, with pain and tears
We thought you'd be there, throughout the years.

Missed deeply by your brother Peter, Elizabeth and your godchild Jamie.

Left: Mary Gough's memorial card. The Gough family made all the funeral arrangements. There is no mention of her husband on the card.
Courtesy of the Gough family

Below: Mary Gough pictured shortly before she died.
Courtesy of the Gough family

Colin Whelan working in the 'Karma Bar' in Porto Portal, Mallorca, on the opening night.
© *Solarpix.com*

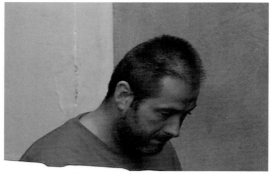

Whelan leaving the Bridewell Court in July 2004, having been extradited from Spain.
Courtesy of the Irish Daily Star on Sunday

By her own admission, she found him to be humorous and able to hold a conversation so she saved him as 'a friend'. He seemed equally interested in her.

A couple of days after her first conversation, she chatted with Celtic Tackle and this time disclosed more information about herself.

Part of this included telling him that her mother had passed away after a battle with cancer.

Whelan wrote back to say he understood her position. Then he went further saying that his own fiancée had died in a car crash seven years previously and that he knew what she was going through.

When Sheppard heard this, she felt she had made a connection with a person who could really understand what she was feeling. She had no idea that Whelan was lying.

'Even though this was only our second conversation I felt that I had made a good friend,' she later recalled.

The gardaí tasked with reading through the emails were stunned. Whelan had invented a new persona for himself to deal with this woman. In one email he even tried to convince Sheppard the photograph was of him.

The relationship developed further. In January, she sent him her mobile telephone number. Whelan pretended not to be too pleased about this development. The following day, he sent her a mail telling her off for sending her mobile phone number over the internet. The killer said he was concerned about her well-being.

If anything, Whelan was a conniving thug. Everything he did was designed to manipulate her emotions. And it worked. Sheppard was genuinely moved by his concern and wrote to him saying so.

The following day, she received a message on her mobile phone sent from Whelan's computer which read, 'tweet tweet, don't fly away little birdy, your number's safe with me, I've sent you mail.'

When she returned home later that day, she received an email from Whelan to say that his father had gone into hospital and that a body scan showed he had a large cyst on his pancreas. This was a lie but Sheppard wasn't to know.

This mail marked the first time that he had spoken about his family. The chat and email continued.

Whelan even compared his father's condition to that of her mother's. Some of the emails upset her and made her cry.

'I felt a lot of empathy for Colin,' she later told the gardaí.

Gradually she began to flirt with him and vice versa. The content of the emails between them became more personal and she would even talk to him about her children.

The inevitable happened towards the end of January when she emailed Whelan and asked if he had ever thought about meeting. He replied saying he had but he was not ready yet.

'I still believed that the photograph Colin had included in his profile was not that of him and that, I believed, was the reason he was avoiding a meeting.'

In February, the relationship became more intense.

'I used to tell him everything about my life and my activities. Colin was now becoming an important part of my life and not only did I speak with him every day via the telephone and internet; I spoke about him to my family and friends. My feelings for Colin were now more than a friend and I told him about this and through his correspondence I could tell he felt the same.'

The garda investigation team garnered that during the first two weeks of February before the murder, Whelan had developed a flirtatious interest in Sheppard.

Prior to Valentine's Day, he asked Sheppard to send him the address of her local florist as he wanted to send her flowers. Their email correspondence resembled those sent by young teenagers.

Whelan would send greeting cards and email correspondence showing bunches of roses or sometimes poems. One email contained a poem entitled 'Mr Bears Ode to a Welsh Bird' and was signed 'Mr Bear xx.'

It read:

Hey Helen I think I may know,
Why I always think of you so,
Whether it's night or whether it's morn,
If my heart feels high or even forlorn,

That feeling doesn't happen too often I admit,
Cause ever since January I've been like a twit,
You see my head rules my heart and it's always been true,
But I don't really mind as long as I have my welsh bird to woo.

I know she's honest and I know she's gentle,
But Jesus at times she drives me damn mental,
You see it's her attitude I think draws me most,
What a laugh I've had recently sending her some post.

But then without forgetting there is some other traits,
That can't go without saying, because she is a good mate,

TILL DEATH DO US PART

No matter what happens, or appears in the future,
I'll always remember that crazy sexy Welsh creature.

I have this image that sometimes appears,
Of a chirpy little bird, beholding its tears,
As majestically it flies from an Irish front door,
With the message of love for all to adore.

I think by times that we are so alike,
Or is it my mind grasping for some light,
Consuming anticipation, second thoughts always appear,
Reflected from my dream, but is the moment near.

Exhaling of old breath, my insecurities conceive fear,
My stomach filled with flutters, Can't believe I'm really
here,
An embrace is made, I lower my face,
Lips touch softly, and Mr Bear's pulses race.

Three whispered words, echo in my furry ear,
Dark hair, long nails, soft tanned cheek and a sliding tear,
Hands reach up, a finger lifts a chin,
Tears brushed away, and both start to grin.

Then reality hits and here comes the banished fear,
Disappointment takes hold, Helen, I'm not really here,
I am but I'm not if you know what I mean,
My surroundings blur, an unbelievable feeling and scene.

Now don't get me wrong Helen I'm very far from sad,
You see sometimes I think too much that that makes me
mad,
Because in my view of life, I know there's always someone
ready to grasp,
The emotions, the people, the things that I decide to let
slip past.

I don't know where all this is coming from but hey it's still
flowing, It must be your presence, your smile, your laugh
it's addictive, I know you said recently that you felt as if you
were back growing,
But all I'll say Helen is you're far from predictive.

That's a compliment to a mum who I've become to
known,
I can picture the traits that her kids have already been
shown,
I'm sure that these kids already know how lucky they are,
To have a mum who cherishes, thinks of and loves them
and not from afar,

Tears from heart nearly fall as I sit and write,
But for once these are tears that I welcome, not fight,
Breathing comes in short and small quick gasps,
They are evidence of my link to you, a link I hold to fast.

I'm not going to question why, I've created this bond.
With this emotional stable Welsh lady who I am so fond,
You never know some day that I wish I may visit,
To the land of the Welsh dragons and most beautiful
people in it.

Well, I come to the end of my long winded mission,
The aim I fully understand at the outset with my decision,
To write a few lines to bring a facial smile to thine,
So until next time Helen, have an excellent Valentine.

Mr Bear.

XX

When she received this mail, Sheppard decided that she wanted to meet Whelan face to face.

'I really wanted to see Colin and finally see a picture of the real man and not the model. From this day on I could not stop thinking of Colin; I could say I was now in love with him,' she later told gardaí.

'I replied to Colin and demanded he send me a photograph of him and this time to send the real one. I did receive correspondence from Colin that included five photographs of himself that he had placed in his profile.'

She cut out the photographs and stuck them to her fridge. Mary had taken the photographs of Whelan while they honeymooned in Thailand. Next she wrote back and told him that she wasn't interested in the model in the picture but that she had fallen for the person who had written to her.

She then sent Whelan a Yahoo greeting entitled 'Lasting Bond' which proclaimed that she was going to take the 'intruder' off her fridge and replace it with his true picture.

She sent an e-card with a picture of a young girl hugging a dog which read as follows:

Promise we'll always be the best of friends.
Awwwww Colin....

How are you feeling, hope not crap. I just want to tell you so much at the moment but I'm hopeless at writing what I feel and anyway you read my mail from the bottom upwards so you won't understand anyway.

Just to let you know I've taken the intruder off my fridge and replaced it with the real furry bear (truth)... thanks..hey, for letting me know. You wouldn't know how much better I feel and I'm sure you do to [sic].

I read all your mail this afternoon, over 50 cards and 20 emails, with your pic here so I can put you together and believe me colin it made more sense to me...I can honestly say that I never thought that was your real pic, I imagined you with dark hair and glasses for some reason.

From this moment on Colin we will become real good friends believe me and if your friends can't forgive you, who will eh.

Why did you think I kept asking for pic, and giving my address I thought...right he will have no excuse...

Really would love to talk to you this weekend furry, so ring me yeah as soon as you can...the sooner the better really...

Eveything I have told you in my mail is true, I am what I am, nothing different, crazy welsh bird who is smitten by a furry dark haired Irishman...so from this moment then Colin all truths yeah...

Talk soon I hope furry, need to speak to you so much, need to hug you so much too..

Your Welsh friend

Helen

x

Reading through his emails, the gardaí were able to deduce that Whelan was a compulsive liar. He fabricated completely bogus stories about himself to garner sympathy. He invented a new persona for himself which he relayed to Sheppard, who took him at his word. The contents of his emails were complete lies.

One email revealed that he claimed he had been married for a total of four months from September 1999 until January 2000.

In that mail, he told Sheppard that his wife had passed away but he did not say how. After she received the mail, Sheppard wrote to Whelan asking him to call. She was worried that she had upset him. Whelan called about 30 minutes later. She asked him if they could meet now and Whelan readily agreed. In this conversation, Sheppard asked him how his wife had died. A liar to the end, he told her that she had died in a crash.

'I sympathised with him and told him that I was there to hold his hand. Colin told me that he felt this and he also told me that at the time of his wife's death he had just started a new job and that his house was under renovation and that it had been a very stressful time. This was the most intense time in the relationship and this came across over the phone. I told him that I was attracted to him although I did not tell him that I loved him.'

Trying to take the relationship further, Sheppard offered to travel to Ireland. Whelan suggested that she visit in April. The gardaí found it difficult to comprehend the sheer volume of emails the two exchanged. In one series, Whelan even wrote to Sheppard helping her to make arrangements for her to stay in Ireland. As always he signed off on each mail as Mr Bear.

The detectives from the Computer Investigation Squad, and later those assigned to the murder hunt, were completely taken aback by Whelan's capacity to lie.

Having read the emails, they were able to see how Whelan could manipulate a relationship simply by inventing fanciful stories. As the time came close for Sheppard to visit Ireland, he simply wrote to her saying he would travel to Wales himself.

As they sifted through the correspondence, they also noticed that Whelan had communicated with Sheppard in the days before he killed Mary.

For example, on Monday, 26 February, at 11am, Sheppard received an email entitled 'Empty Arms' and this gave details about him being in Germany and that he would not be back in Dublin until the following Tuesday or Wednesday. This email was sent on 26 February, as he made final preparations to murder Mary. In it he claimed to be travelling in Germany. He wrote about German culture, compared the locals to androids and even remarked about the way German women dressed.

Right well I'm gonna have to go for the moment and face the world of German clothes shops to get a couple of things, this should be fun..clothes taste is up their ass, well it must be seeing some of the dischevelled [*sic*] looking individuals arriving in here, not that I'm any Valentino myself or anything far from it believe me...but I think Homer Simpson ties went out just a while ago and thank Christ I never possessed one....probably offending you now, yeah I know you think they look fine (not).....ahhhhh. C'mon can you tell me the last time someone wore a tank top and a shirt and tie...No...well, I'll tell you there's a few over here who think they look the dogs....as they say and believe me they do look like the dogs....ahhhhhhhhhh wake up androids.

Right I'm away, I'll drop you a few lines later on hopefully, if I don't get too excited here and maybe have 2 beers instead of the average 1.67 litres per person.................well take it easy anyhow and enjoy the last revel...Hey you're all choclattly....mmmmmmmm
Cya
Furry
Hey, just got into hotmail to send this and noticed I've 2 mails, gonna send this first anyway Ok...don't want to revise all of the above in the light of what you may tell me in the other ones...Ahhh You know what I mean...I'll read the other mails then Ok...Oh yeah mail me your phone number cause it's in my mobile and that's well gone, god knows where it is...ah c'mon don't make me beg for it.... ruff, ruff, get off ma back, you mad thing....

Sheppard had no idea he was writing from his office in St Stephen's Green. She had no way of knowing.

Now in the throes of love, she wrote to him saying that she wanted him to come to Wales as soon as possible.

Whelan telephoned later that night and even spoke at length about the area he said he was in.

'By now without a shadow of a doubt I can say that I really loved him,' she said later.

The last email she received from Whelan was sent at lunch time on 28 February—hours before he murdered his wife. In it, Whelan opened up and expressed what Sheppard interpreted as personal feelings. He phoned a couple of hours later and spoke for about a half an hour about the content of his previous email. He said he was still in Germany and would not be returning until Thursday. That was the last time Sheppard ever heard from Whelan.

The evidence seized from Whelan's computer proved beyond all reasonable doubt that the gardaí had identified the killer. Whelan wasn't simply a man who engaged in extramarital affairs behind his wife's back; he was something more sinister. He was capable of living several lives at any one time.

More importantly, he was a man capable of lying about anything.

Gallagher stepped up his investigation telling his officers to prepare to make an arrest.

~ ~ ~

Two days after the investigation team seized Whelan's computer, the body of Mary Gough was released for burial. It was a horrific experience for her family. Whelan didn't get involved in the funeral preparations more out of fear than anything else. The Gough family arranged the undertaker.

'He never asked me, "Are you able?" or anything. He didn't take over the burial, he handed it over to us,' Marie recalled.

Marie had no qualms about consulting Whelan on the arrangements. In fact, she made a point of keeping a line of communication with him open, if only to embarrass him and make him know the heartache that he had caused. But Whelan was intimidated by this.

'I rang him up and he said, "Oh, no problem," that's the answer I got from him. That was the last time I spoke to him.'

The truth was that Marie felt she had lost everything. She couldn't contemplate a life without her beloved Mary. This was noticed by the gardaí hunting the killer, who were more than sympathetic to her plight. Not able to offer any real comfort and knowing that Whelan was capable of anything, members of the investigation team arranged for her to gain access to Mary's home before Whelan got the keys back. Judging by the contents of his emails, they knew he was more than capable of erasing what little was left of Mary's life out of existence.

Accompanied by a garda and two of Mary's friends, she returned to the house five days after Mary was strangled. It was a heart-breaking experience for her.

'The gardaí told us we could go in and take some personal stuff. So I went in with two of the girls. When I went into the house, it was dead. You'd think someone switched off an inner light; it didn't even look the same. There was this dull cold atmosphere.

'We got a few ornaments that some of the lads had given her, we got her clothes and her shoes and anything to do with her that we could see.

'We went upstairs to the bedroom and there were pieces of the carpet taken away, bits of the saddle board were gone and bits of wallpaper had been taken off the wall. There was nothing taken from the stairs so I knew she definitely didn't fall down the stairs. The gloom of the place was dreadful,' she recalled.

A week after Mary was brutally murdered; her body was finally brought to the church where she had married six months previously.

Now she lay in St Patrick's Church, a couple of hundred yards from her family home, her life cut short at the hands of the man she loved.

The small village of Stamullen was thronged with the friends and family of Mary for her funeral. The church was packed to capacity as people tried to pay their last respects to a girl everyone loved.

But there was tension in the air. One person stood out from among the crowd. It was Whelan. He had insisted on attending the service despite the fact that it was common knowledge that he had murdered his wife. His family, of course, had no idea that he was the killer and also turned out to pay their respects. They were all genuinely heartbroken over Mary's death but this was of little consolation to the Gough family. Rather than get into a confrontation with Whelan, Mary's immediate family sat to one side of the church.

'We were all together and he was over on the other side of the church. Usually the families would all be together but he stayed on the other side with his family.'

She recalls that the mourners were all stunned when they saw Whelan in attendance.

'The poor priest only married them six months beforehand. Normally, the coffin is placed to the left in the church and all the next of kin are all behind, but the priest didn't want to put her either side so he put her in on the altar. Mary would have definitely been laughing her head off at this.'

Mary was finally laid to rest in the adjoining cemetery by her family and friends. The atmosphere at the funeral became hostile when Whelan showed visible signs of emotion.

Many observers watched in disbelief as he hijacked the ceremony, acting out the role of a young, bereaved husband. The Gough's, however, kept their dignity and ignored him.

But more tragedy was to befall the Gough family that very same day.

On the day of the funeral, Marie's 80-year-old father died while Mary was being buried. No one told her until after her daughter's funeral had ended.

She was first told that her father was not well and that he had been brought to the hospital. She rushed to the hospital after burying Mary but was told when she arrived that he had tragically died.

'He knew Mary was dead but we told him that she had fallen down the stairs. On Monday after, someone was in the house with him. He asked why they weren't burying Mary and said that there was something funny going on; that something funny happened in Balbriggan. He was 80 but he was a young 80. He knew something had happened.'

Two days later Marie buried her father. She recalls that period of her life as one of the hardest.

Within days of the funeral, Whelan returned to normal. Having faced the public at his dead wife's funeral, he decided to stop acting and get on with his life. He had convinced himself that he had committed the perfect crime because he had not been arrested.

Once he was finished with the pretences, he sent word to Mary's brother Peter to come to Clonard Street. He said he had something to give him.

'I do not know exactly where Colin was ringing from but I suspected it was from 49 Clonard Street. Colin said, "There are a few bags of Mary's belongings in the house if you want to come and collect them."

'I said I would call at 7pm on my way to my mother's. That was the end of the conversation.'

When he rang the doorbell, Whelan answered the door while holding the cat.

Peter couldn't help but notice the carpet was missing from the hall, the stairs and sitting-room. Whelan dispensed with the pleasantries and invited him into the kitchen where he pointed to three plastic bags on the kitchen table.

Peter would later tell gardaí, 'He told me Mary's stuff was in the bags. He said, "There is nothing else in the house belonging to her except a bike in the shed which you can collect whenever."

'I just picked up the bags and left. I was only in the house for about four minutes or so.'

Whelan acted as if nothing had happened. He was wiping Mary from his life. He kept nothing belonging to her.

When Peter opened the bag, he found the remainder of Mary's belongings. In one bag there was Mary's toothbrush and a mouse mat with a picture of a cat.

Another bag contained a prized leather jacket. When Marie had entered the house with the gardaí after the funeral, she had seen two black AA jackets that both Mary and Whelan wore while attending motor rallies.

Not knowing which belonged to Mary, she left them there. Whelan and Mary had bought the jackets in Tallaght years earlier when the Circuit of Ireland rally stage stopped there. Peter could not believe that Whelan had given away the jacket. More importantly, he was struck by Whelan's cold manner.

'He was so indifferent to me, how I felt, my family, how they felt. It was as if nothing had happened,' he said later.

Before he left, Whelan asked him about Mary's jewellery box and about £800 he said was in it. Hurt and upset, Peter told him that the Garda had it.

'That's all I said and I left.'

When Marie examined the contents of the bags, she couldn't believe his brazenness. Whelan was wiping the remains of Mary out of his life and was already making plans to rent out the property.

He then moved back to Gormanstown much to Marie's surprise.

'So we never got back into the house again and if we had known that we would have brought a lorry; Mary had some lovely things.'

CHAPTER 7

Gallagher's team worked round the clock to gather intelligence on Whelan and his modus operandi. His computer had given them a treasure trove of good intelligence. There were also the results of Mary's post-mortem and other forensics. Samples of carpet and clothes taken from the scene had been examined by scientists attached to the State Forensic Laboratory in Garda Headquarters.

They had also talked to Helen Sheppard. On the afternoon of Mary's funeral, a Welsh policeman named DC Phil Simmonds of Tonypundy CID called to Sheppard at her home. He asked if she knew

Colin Whelan. Sheppard said she did and asked if something had happened to him. Simmonds came straight to the point and told her the gardaí wanted to ask her about her relationship with Whelan and the suspicious death of his wife. Sheppard nearly collapsed because she believed Mary had died in a car crash over a year ago. She offered to help in any way she could and testify if necessary.

But more than anything else, the investigation team was still intrigued as to the motive behind the murder. This soon became apparent.

Discreet investigations by the gardaí in the days after the death revealed that Whelan had taken out a ten-year £400,000 (€500,000) insurance policy on his wife's life just three months before they married.

Whelan first set this plan in action in March 2000 when he was approved for a £200,000 insurance policy but then sought to double this policy stating that he was a self-employed IT consultant. Irish Life without hesitation approved the increased insurance policy as, on paper, Whelan and Mary were a young, affluent couple combined with a low risk.

But if either Whelan or Mary were to die, there would be a £400,000 pay out. Therefore, if Whelan could make Mary's death look like an accident, he would stand to benefit a lot of money.

When the investigation team began checking out the background of his insurance policy, they discovered that as Mary went for fittings for her wedding dress and picked out flowers for her big day, Whelan spent his time working out how much her life was worth. This was the ultimate betrayal; Mary was marrying for love, Whelan was marrying for money.

The investigation revealed that on 2 May, a new life policy application was forwarded to the new business section of Irish Life insurance company. The policy was made out in the name of Colin Whelan and Mary Gough with an address at 49 Clonard Street, Balbriggan, Co. Dublin.

This proposal form was checked over and was found to be in order and properly signed by Colin Whelan and his wife, Mary. It was assigned policy number 6317584 and was dated 2 May 2000 headed with the name Colin Whelan. Details of the policy were entered into an electronic underwriting system, which was reviewed by personnel in the underwriting department at Irish Life who decided whether or not to approve the policy.

The next day, a senior underwriter at Irish Life received the proposal and approved it for £400,000 life cover on both lives of Mary Gough and Colin Whelan at standard rates. The level of cover of £400,000 was higher than Irish Life's average sum assured, however, on assessing the client's situation it was deemed within acceptable limits.

Whelan had explained that he worked in the IT sector and given the economic background in 2000 was likely to be on a high income. Generally for a person of that age, insurers would allow up to ten to fifteen times income as an acceptable level of cover and usually allow a similar level of cover on the partner.

On accepting the proposal the application form was returned to Irish Life to issue the policy documents.

The first payment of £51.24 was made in June 2000 and the payments continued thereafter.

Irish Life co-operated fully with the gardaí. The company revealed that Whelan had initially contacted Irish Life in a phone call to customer services the previous March.

As is standard practice, a proposal form was sent out. Whelan returned the application form with completed questionnaires for medical purposes.

The documents were signed by both Mary and Whelan himself. But when the documents were posted back, Irish Life discovered that he had enclosed a letter indicating that he required dual life cover of £400,000 instead of £200,000. He stated in this letter that the initial quote value of £200,000 would not be sufficient, partly because he was self-employed and he requested a quotation for the revised amount.

The gardaí learned that Whelan was contacted when the letter was received and informed that the new premium would be £56.31 but this was later adjusted to £51.24 payable by direct debit.

Irish Life had retained the relevant records and were able to show that on 9 May, Whelan rang Irish Life once more asking them to activate the policy.

The company did as instructed. The couple were considered to be of minimal risk and also the fact that the policy was for a ten-year term meant that the proposal was accepted without further investigation and life cover issued on 1 June 2000.

When the gardaí examined the file, they discovered that Mary had not been involved in increasing her own life insurance. Her husband to be had done everything.

What's more the death benefit payable was now £400,000 and the beneficiary was one Colin Whelan.

~ ~ ~

Meanwhile, Whelan managed to convince himself that he had committed the perfect crime. He dispensed with all pleasantries to the Gough family. He made it clear that he no longer wanted to see them or retain any memories of Mary. As for the gardaí, he had nothing but utter contempt for them. And he figured that if they had any hard evidence he would have been arrested. That was his fatal mistake.

The truth was that Gallagher had decided to gather more than enough evidence before making an arrest. Behind the scenes, the enquiry team worked day and night sifting through Whelan's personal emails, his correspondence with Sheppard and his internet trawls for information on asphyxiation.

The gardaí had a distinct advantage on him because they knew he was the killer. And the best evidence of all was the post-mortem report which stated that Mary had been strangled. Whelan had also signed a statement on the night of the murder saying he was the only other person in the house that fatal night. When the enquiry team discovered that Whelan had increased his wife's life insurance, they had uncovered his motive.

In the space of a week, Gallagher's team had compiled a dossier of damning evidence which showed Whelan to be a liar, a fantasist and a person fixated on strangulation.

After several debriefing sessions where all the evidence was assembled and examined, Gallagher gave the order to arrest Whelan. It was now time to turn up the heat.

~ ~ ~

At 8.20am, on the morning of Tuesday, 10 April, Detective Richard Culhane accompanied by Sergeant Denis Murphy, descended on Whelan's family home. They were accompanied by 12 gardaí and were armed with a search warrant.

They knocked at the door but Whelan didn't answer. Instead his mother Olive opened the door and spoke with the gardaí who explained the purpose of the visit.

On entering the house, Culhane walked directly into Whelan's bedroom. He found Whelan lying awake in bed. The killer looked stunned but tried to conceal his nerves by being smart when Sgt Patrick Marry also walked into the room and introduced himself.

'I know who you are,' was all he said.

Whelan then got up, dressed and walked into the sitting-room to get his shoes.

At this stage he was still not formally under arrest. This led him to conclude that the gardaí had just obtained a search warrant to search his home as part of a general trawl. He thought this was nothing more than a shakedown.

This myth was dispelled moments later when Sgt Marry followed him into the sitting-room. Walking over to the killer, Sgt Marry put his hand on Whelan's shoulder and said he was arresting him on suspicion of the murder of his wife, Mary Whelan between 28 February and 1 March 2001 at 49 Clonard Street, Balbriggan.

On hearing the words, Whelan went as white as a ghost.

Marry continued, 'You are not obliged to say anything unless you wish to do so and anything you do say will be taken down in writing and may be given in evidence.'

Whelan stood there speechless. He had never imagined this day would come. He was stunned and not knowing what else to do, he remained silent. He was no longer in control of the game.

Culhane, Marry and Detective Peter McCoy took him to a waiting patrol car which transported him to Balbriggan Garda Station. Once his custody record was completed and he was processed, it was time for Whelan to face the music.

At this time, he had no notion as to what the enquiry team did and didn't know. This put him at an obvious disadvantage. Unlike the detectives who had spent the previous 48 hours planning out the questions they wanted him to answer, he was caught by surprise.

With no time to lose, the first interrogation began at 8.55am that same morning and was led by Detective Michael Considine and Detective John Clancy. They were armed with a list of 50 specific questions.

However, Whelan was in no mood for a confession. The reality of the situation that he now found himself trapped in became too much. Although he was stunned and shocked at the mere notion that he had been arrested, he was worried. Rather than incriminate himself any further, he dispensed with all pleasantries.

The interrogation began with a series of simple questions. Whelan was asked if his earlier statement had been correct. He said it was.

Considine then asked him, 'Do you want to change anything in it now, having thought about this?'

Whelan replied, 'No, that's what happened.'

The gardaí didn't need a fortune teller to know that Whelan had no intention of pleading guilty and telling the truth. But once they had given him the opportunity to come clean, the real interrogation began.

They began by asking him a series of questions which established that he was the only person in the house with his wife when she died. Given that the post-mortem had concluded that she was strangled, Whelan's answers actually incriminated himself.

'Were you at home on your own that night Colin?'

'Mary was there,' he said.

'Yes, but did anyone else call or visit the house that night?'

'No, my sister rang, that was all, nobody called to the house,' he retorted.

The two gardaí probed further but Whelan had already realised his mistake. When they asked him another seemingly irrelevant question, he refused to say another word. Caught in a blind panic, Whelan started to lose his nerve.

The gardaí asked him more questions. Each and every one were designed to make him contradict his earlier statements.

The first lie they asked him about was his claims that Mary had scratched his chest while dying.

'Can you account for saying that Mary grabbed you? How did that happen?'

'She grabbed me,' said Whelan.

'How did this happen?'

'She clutched me with her right hand,' he added.

'What did you mean by saying she struggled?'

Realising his mistake, he reverted to saying, 'I've no comment.'

'Do you remember talking to the fireman on the telephone? He told you about CPR, is that right?'

'Yep,' he replied.

'Did he tell you to keep Mary warm?' asked the detective.

'I've no comment.'

Whelan knew where this line of questioning was going. What's more, he knew he was in trouble. He had no answer to the questions because there was none he could give.

The gardaí continued to fire questions at him. They asked him about everything that he had previously said about Mary's death and pointed out each and every contradiction in the story. Nothing made sense, they said.

Eventually they asked him straight out to tell the truth but Whelan remained silent.

It is crucial in difficult interrogations to keep suspects talking; even about banal matters like the weather or sport. This helps build a bond between the interviewer and the interviewee. Fearing that Whelan would clam up altogether, the gardaí often switched their lines of questioning.

At one point, they asked him why he had refused to let a priest see Mary when she died. The ploy worked, Whelan opened up again.

'That's not my understanding.'

'What's your understanding?'

'I remember being asked for a priest, I did not want one. It was not obvious to me that it was for my wife.'

Whelan met with his solicitor around 10am and sought legal advice. When the interview resumed, the gardaí began pressing him to explain why he had told people that he hadn't been charged with a crime.

'Were you expecting to be arrested Colin?'

'I've no comment.'

'Did that sleeve become ripped when Mary was struggling with you?'

'I've no comment.'

When these questions failed to elicit any meaningful responses, the two detectives moved to others subject including some bizarre conversations where Whelan spoke about strangulation. The gardaí quoted various people whom Whelan had discussed strangulation with.

They even quoted Whelan's words from one such conversation.

'You said, "What do they mean strangulation; do they mean strangulation with an item of clothing, manual strangulation or asphyxiation?" Did you say this?'

Whelan stared away without saying as much as a word prompting his interrogator to proclaim, 'We have gone through the different stories you have told. There is no break-in and nobody else in the house, only you and your wife. How did you wife get strangled?'

There was nothing but silence from the killer.

Finally they asked, 'Why did you strangle her Colin?'

Whelan stared ahead and said not a word.

The two gardaí left the interrogation room in accordance with regulations. Before they left, Whelan was handed a copy of the interview notes which he signed and was allowed to rest.

The first interrogation team had not mentioned any of the secret intelligence that had been obtained from the computer. The carefully selected questions asked in the first interview were designed to make him think that the gardaí had only the post-mortem results to work on.

But that afternoon, Insp Dominic Hayes, attached to the National Bureau of Criminal Investigation, prepared to enter the interrogation room with a fellow detective, Pat Flood.

Earlier that morning, Hayes had received a printout of telephone calls made from Whelan's mobile and work telephones to his online girlfriend Helen Sheppard, along with details of the internet searches Whelan had conducted.

Armed with these documents, Hayes and Flood began to question Whelan.

They first asked him about his relationship with Mary whom he said he loved very much. Whelan proclaimed they were happy and that he was never violent towards her. In fact, he went further, saying they never exchanged a cross word.

Their marriage was one of happiness. According to Whelan, his was a loving marriage and one that he treasured. He also stated that he had never had an affair, or ever sought any kind of relationship outside marriage.

He said their sex life was normal and satisfying and that he never had to look for anything outside their marriage, sex or otherwise. Hayes said no more.

Directing the interrogation, he asked Whelan about his work with Irish Permanent.

The inspector handed Whelan a floor plan of his office in the Irish Permanent building prompting Whelan to point out where he sat. The garda next asked him about his username for logging onto the computer which Whelan said was unique to him. They spoke about his job and Whelan let it slip that he was aware they had seized his computer at work.

Hayes made no particular remark about this but then produced two pictures. Whelan looked at the pictures which were of him on honeymoon on an island off the coast of Thailand.

Hayes looked Whelan straight in the eye and asked if he knew where the gardaí got them. Cocky to the core, Whelan said 'Off the web.'

Hayes then asked if he was Celtic Tackle.

The remark knocked Whelan for six. He was dumbstruck and could think of nothing to say.

Hayes pressed him again asking if he was Celtic Tackle prompting Whelan to reply, 'It's obvious it's a name I used on the web.'

Hayes slowly started producing tidbits of information about Whelan's correspondence with Sheppard. This panicked Whelan.

He produced a printout of a greeting card he had received from Sheppard on the day Mary was killed. He asked Whelan if he remembered it. Lost for words, the killer could only say 'yes.'

Whelan didn't need a fortune teller to tell him the investigation team knew about his online romance. Trying to regain some control, he decided to come clean about Sheppard figuring it could do no harm. After all he hadn't ever met her.

He went on to say that he had been communicating with her on the internet and had spoken to her on the phone. Like a fool, he admitted that she called him 'Furry Bear' and he called her 'Welsh Bird.'

Wondering what reaction he would get, Hayes next produced bound copies of all the emails and greeting cards sent by Sheppard to him. Whelan nodded as Hayes turned each page slowly to confirm they were his.

Not wanting to lose the momentum, Hayes next produced an album of photos Sheppard had sent him.

Now with Whelan on the back foot, Hayes asked him where he saw the relationship going.

'I don't know,' said Whelan.

Hayes appeared to be genuinely intrigued. Whelan was by now in a state of panic. If the gardaí had his emails, was it possible they also had details about his internet searches on strangulation.

Meanwhile, Hayes continued to ask about the relationship. More to the point, he asked Whelan why he lied about his own situation and when he planned to meet Sheppard. Whelan just blurted out the word 'no'.

Stunned and rattled, he scrambled to gather his thoughts and said he couldn't remember what he had told her.

Whelan was now on the ropes. Hayes saw the opportunity and suggested that he and Sheppard were like two 14-year-olds in love. This time Whelan just nodded his head and agreed.

The next piece of evidence presented to the killer caused him to turn crimson with embarrassment. It was the poem he wrote Sheppard, 'Ode to a Welsh bird' and the letter 'Oh Helen, Helen, Helen.' Whelan had no option but to confess to the online affair at least. What he didn't realise was that Hayes was now controlling the interview. Sensing Whelan's distressed state, Hayes proceeded to ask him why he had claimed that he was in Germany when talking to Sheppard. This was odd behaviour.

Whelan held his head down. He was forced to admit the whole story was a lie.

The two gardaí noted a change in Whelan from that moment. He was talking openly and honestly for the first time. His body language was that of a man embarrassed.

Hayes didn't relent. He next presented Whelan with a copy of the email that he had signed 'Furry' which he sent to Sheppard to discuss suitable times and dates for his planned trip to Cardiff.

'She was pushing to meet. I was putting her off.'

Which led Hayes to ask, if this was the case, why had he looked up bookings for the Hilton Hotel in Cardiff?

This sent Whelan into a state of panic. He now knew the officers had obtained precise details on his internet searches though he dared not say it.

'I don't know why I did that,' he replied. 'She was looking to come across and I was putting her off,' he said.

Whelan then tried to lie by saying that he had first made contact with Sheppard 'some time after Christmas' but that he wasn't sure.

Hayes contradicted him immediately and read out an email from that January in which he said that his wife was dead. He asked him about this.

'I didn't want her to know I was married. I wanted her to think I was single,' answered Whelan.

Despite everything, Whelan continued to claim that he never intended to meet Sheppard face to face. Why then, was he looking up property in Wales, Hayes enquired.

'I don't know why.'

Hayes then asked why he had offered Sheppard the use of his spare room.

'Yes, but it wasn't going to happen,' he said.

If that was so, Hayes suggested, why then had he arranged to see Sheppard on the weekend of 2 March. Again Whelan repeated, 'yes, but it wasn't going to happen.'

Whelan said he was not in love with Sheppard but that she certainly loved him.

Hayes then came straight out and told Whelan that he killed his wife Mary so he could be with Sheppard.

'I didn't kill Mary.'

Who killed her then, Hayes asked.

'No comment,' was Whelan's answer.

The gardaí were now in full control of the interview. Whelan was in a complete state. They could see that he was agitated and terrified. In his own mind, he knew the game was up. He had never expected them to get that far.

Hayes wasn't about to stop now. For tactical reasons, he switched the line of interrogation to other women who Whelan had contacted over the internet. He made reference to Tina and Linda. He asked Whelan if he remembered looking up Tina's Irish roots for her.

'That's right; I looked it up for her.'

Why, if he was happily married, Hayes put it to him, was he communicating with women and advertising himself on the internet. Whelan answered, 'I never met anybody' prompting the interrogator to ask aloud was it because nobody answered.

'No comment,' he replied.

This was a clever diversion. Once Whelan's concentration was elsewhere, Hayes returned to the subject of Mary's murder. He took him through the days events. He talked about how the gardaí knew he had gone to work as normal, bought Mary a gift in Brown Thomas and then spoke to Sheppard before calling Mary in Wade's.

Whelan nodded in agreement with the timeline of events but said he couldn't remember the conversation he had with Sheppard.

Hayes then looked him straight in the eye and asked him about why he searched the internet for information on 'loss of consciousness' that afternoon.

Whelan went white and replied, 'no comment.'

He then blurted out that someone else could have accessed the information.

Hayes handed him a computer printout which showed the five sites he had visited.

Flood began questioning him at this point. He produced a 1997 diary he had seized from Whelan's office desk and asked if it was his diary. At first Whelan said 'no comment' and then said he owned it.

Flood leafed through the diary until he came to a page that listed numbers for dating services. He asked Whelan if he had used the service at any stage.

'No, I didn't meet anyone from it.'

This line of questioning was tactical. It was to prelude a much more serious set of questions. Without warning, Hayes asked Whelan why he searched the internet for information on 'death by strangulation' and visited the site of 'North Carolina's Lawyers Weekly.'

Hayes put it down for the record that the website covered the case of Henry Lewis Wallace, who had strangled nine women. Whelan said 'no comment' as he shook with fear. Seeing his opportunity, Hayes put it to Whelan that he was the killer. He said he had accessed the sites to get information to help with his aim to strangle his wife.

He told Whelan that he knew he had searched for information on 'death by strangulation' on the internet six days before his wife was strangled. When Whelan replied 'no comment', they asked him if he was denying that he accessed the sites. Ever the fool, Whelan mumbled, 'I'm not denying it.'

The gardaí had made a breakthrough. Whelan had begun to crack. They hit him with more evidence causing him to stutter and mumble his words. They put it to him that on 20 February, he had accessed information on how to block the windpipe and also visited the sites of www. genocide.com.

This time he didn't even bother denying it.

'I must have.'

They next asked him why he had surfed the internet later that same day for information on how long it took for people to die from asphyxia.

'Probably, I must have done. I don't recall but it must have been me.'

The gardaí threw the proverbial book at him; the expert interrogators pressed him further. They asked him repeatedly about why he searched the internet using the terms 'lack of oxygen to the brain' amongst others.

'I can't recall.'

It went on and on.

Hayes now came straight to the point. There was only one reason why he had searched those sites. He said it was to get information to help in his desire to kill his wife by strangulation.

Whelan held his head in his hands and looked at the floor before saying 'no comment.'

Embarrassing Whelan further, Hayes and Flood let the suspect know that they knew everything. They mentioned that he was due to meet Sheppard shortly after his wife's murder; that he had sought information on 'instant death' and 'extramarital affairs' to which he answered, 'I can't recall visiting that.'

The list of damning evidence they had was endless.

Hayes produced an Irish Pen Pal profile headed 'Irish male, 29 seeks E-pals worldwide' along with other searches conducted on five separate dates that January. Hayes asked Whelan if he had posted the advert himself. Whelan said he had.

Finally they put it to him that he was the killer and he searched the net for information to help him murder his wife Mary. For the last time, Whelan replied 'no comment' but this time refused to sign the garda notes.

The killer knew the game was up.

CHAPTER 8

There is no doubt that he knew he was going to be charged with the murder of his wife, yet despite the mounting evidence he continued to protest his innocence. In his own mind, he felt he had no other option. No matter what happened, no matter what evidence the gardaí produced about his online relationship and fascination with strangulation, Whelan had no intention of making a confession. It was beyond him.

The reality of his situation was that the gardaí had a watertight case. Whelan knew it was over but he couldn't admit it to himself. He had gone too far in the deception; so far he couldn't turn back. There was no way out.

Later that evening, he began another round of interviews. This time, the gardaí wanted to introduce evidence which they felt was necessary to secure a murder charge.

At around 7.05pm, Clancy and Considine returned to the interview room at Balbriggan Garda Station. Whelan was still trying to work out how he was going to cope with a court appearance. He had dared the gardaí to charge him if they had any evidence when talking about Mary's death. Now he figured they were about to do just that.

What he didn't know was that the enquiry team now had all the pieces to the jigsaw and knew what had motivated him—money.

Considine began the interview by telling the killer that he was still investigating the murder of his wife and cautioned him once again. This time they came straight to the point and asked Whelan about the insurance policy he took out with Irish Life.

Whelan was taken aback. When he heard the question, he knew the game was up. Rather than act startled, he decided not to ignore the question and answered it as best he could. He said he took the policy out and that it covered both his and Mary's life for £400,000. He made no bones about the fact that he initially asked for a policy for £200,000 but had increased it to £400,000. The policy, he told the detectives, was to cover either of them dying and was payable only on the death of either of them.

'I was aware I was getting married to Mary in September and that I would benefit from her will if she died and likewise if I died,' he said.

Whelan may have studied the intricacies of strangulation but not the law. When he didn't contest this evidence and admitted to what he'd done, the gardaí had him.

The two detectives then returned to Sheppard. Whelan was a little more forthcoming this time. He spoke openly about the relationship saying, 'the reason for the relationship via the internet with Helen Sheppard was for no particular reason. I didn't want a serious relationship. I kept putting her off about meeting.'

When they asked if Mary knew about the relationship of sorts, Whelan said he hadn't told her.

'She knew nothing about it,' he added.

This particular interview was aimed at putting various parts of the prosecution's case to Whelan for the record. In this regard, the gardaí pressed him to answer more questions about his fascination with strangulation. While Whelan felt he could explain his relationship with Sheppard, there was no logical explanation for his dark fascination with strangulation. This was something that was not easily explained. Even Whelan, who was at times delusional, knew this.

'You accessed the computer on January 2 at 2.42pm and followed up with search on choking at 2.47pm, another search on smothering at 4.07pm and again at 4.09pm. You searched blocking the air supply at 4.10pm and opened page G.WINNET health system. What did you look at that page? Were you doing a medical course?'

Whelan refused to answer the question but this didn't perturb the gardaí. This interrogation was, in garda terms, a mop-up. The officers were putting various types of questions to the suspect in case they became pertinent in months to come. These were just a formality before Whelan was formally charged.

The next question switched to forensic evidence found at the house.

'I asked you earlier about blood on your hands or face and about blood on the telephone and the carpet and stairway, do you remember that?' asked Considine.

'Yes.'

Whelan was next shown some exhibits. These were the items that he used to kill Mary. Whelan hadn't seen these since the night that he took Mary's life. He tried not to express any emotion when they were laid out before him.

The first item handed to him was a check-coloured shirt which had blood on the left-hand side and was found by gardaí on the landing of Clonard Street.

The interrogators pointed out minute blood spots on the sleeves, near the cuffs. Whelan was asked what he had to say about this.

He was next shown part of a wooden saddle board with small blood stains. This was very important evidence. The wood had been taken from the doorway between his bedroom and landing. One of the gardaí pointed out the blood stains and asked him to explain how the bloodstains got on it. Again, he said 'no comment.'

The presence of blood on the skirting board categorically proved that a violent altercation had taken place in the bedroom. If Mary had really died after she had fallen down the stairs, there would have been no blood left on the route she took to the stairs. Whelan hadn't thought of this.

He was then shown a navy and white stripped dressing gown with a belt. Whelan had no problem in saying the gown was his. He seemed confused at the line of questioning. When the gardaí asked if he had worn the gown on the night of Mary's death, he refused to answer the question. He suspected an ambush and he was right.

The detectives next produced an evidence bag that contained the belt of his dressing gown. The gardaí pointed out that it had bloodstains on the back of it.

Whelan looked straight ahead, trying not to get emotional. Asked how he could account for these stains being there and, in particular, at the back of the belt, he said he had no comment to make.

The gardaí were now letting him know they had everything. Ever the fool, he thought he had planned everything to the last detail but had forgotten about his computers, emails and the items that he used to murder Mary. The gardaí wanted him to know the game was over and that he was going to jail.

They also introduced Mary's missing wedding ring at this point. She hadn't been wearing any rings on arrival at A&E in Beaumont Hospital, but the forensic team later found her wedding ring at the bottom of the stairs in Clonard Street. This would indicate that her ring had come off her during a struggle. Whelan, once again, had no answer for them.

The detectives then asked him a question that made him tremble. They asked him directly if he had removed the belt of his dressing gown at any time on the night his wife died.

'No comment,' he replied.

He was then shown his wife's white, teddy bear pyjamas. They were bloodied in parts. He had nothing to say about this. He said he didn't know how the blood got on them.

Whelan was now in a state of mental panic. He knew he hadn't a hope; he looked like a caged animal. His confidence had evaporated; it had left him. His body language was that of a frightened man. Some of the enquiry team wondered what Mary would say if she could see him now.

He had spent months planning her murder. He had studied strangulation. He had prepared himself to kill and carried out the gruesome task without difficulty. He had never doubted his own capability to kill. He saw himself as someone who was super intelligent and brighter than others.

If everything had worked out, he would have pocketed £400,000—a tidy sum to restart his new life. Now it all lay in tatters. He had deluded himself.

He knew this, as did the detectives who sensed they were winning. And that he was about to crumble.

They next turned their attention to the internet searches he had conducted from his work computer.

He was asked why he read about the serial killer Wallace and why he read about the use of a towel in aiding or disguising ligature marks in manual strangulation.

'Is that why the towel was found up in the front of your wife's neck?' one detective asked.

Whelan couldn't bring himself to even try to answer this question.

'No comment,' was his response.

Now it was time to remind him of the stupidity he displayed in Beaumont Hospital when he allowed Dr Unadiae to examine the scratch marks on his body. He never could explain how he had sustained the injuries. For all his cunning, Whelan had shown himself to be a fool, albeit a dangerous and sinister one.

Finally the gardaí decided to reveal the contents of the post-mortem report carried out on Mary's body. This was read out to Whelan, and the gardaí stated without fear of contradiction that the cause of death was asphyxiation with the use of a ligature. The gardaí eye-balled Whelan one last time and asked him what he had to say. Sensing his own demise, he could only muster up two words.

'No comment.'

Considine read back over the contents of the interview but Whelan refused to sign them once more. This didn't matter; they all knew the interview marked the end of the road. Whelan was about to be exposed for what he was.

Just after 10am the following morning, Colin Whelan was taken from Balbriggan Garda Station in a patrol car to Swords District Court by Culhane and other members of the investigation team.

Before he left, the killer had asked for a change of clothing to be provided. He chose to wear a dark suit with a patterned tie. Appearances meant everything to the psychotic killer.

He reached the court building around 10.25am and stepped out of the car, flanked by detectives.

He managed to hold himself together for the case and didn't break down crying. He never looked around to see who was present. Instead, he kept his eyes on the ground as he tried to contemplate his next move. The truth was that he couldn't think straight. He had barely slept the night before, knowing that his life as he knew it was about to end.

People wanted to see him brought to justice. Many had found his devil may care attitude to his wife's murder stomach churning. Although Whelan had forgotten about Mary, others hadn't. No one sympathised with him. No one cared. He was a ruthless killer and now it was payback time.

The hearing itself lasted no more than five minutes and Whelan was treated like any other common criminal. When the charges were formally read out to him, all he said was, 'I didn't do it.'

When the court procedure ended, Whelan was brought to Cloverhill Prison where Sgt Marry lodged him in custody on foot of a warrant issued earlier by the judge at Swords District Court. His prison stay was not to be long.

Later that afternoon, his lawyers went to the High Court and appealed against the ruling made earlier in Swords District Court. Whelan was unexpectedly released on bail that afternoon. He paid some of it himself, and an independent surety was provided by his brother-in-law, Jimmy Brassil. However, he was asked to surrender his passport and instructed to report twice a week to his local garda station in Balbriggan. Under the terms of his release by the High Court, he was forbidden to contact anyone connected with the case. Whelan readily agreed to all the terms and walked away a free man, much to the disbelief of the Gough family and Mary's close friends.

CHAPTER 9

For Colin Whelan, watching the public reaction to his appearance in court on charges of murdering his wife was agonising. Whelan's entire personality was built on respectability; that was now gone. Although he hadn't been convicted for the murder; in the public's mind he was no innocent man.

When he was released on bail, he soon discovered that few people wanted to know him. His neighbours avoided him. Local people even crossed the road when they saw him coming.

He had never anticipated any of this. He also lost his job at Irish Permanent, having worked there for nine years. He took this hard; his career had meant everything to him.

He soon found out that the only people who still wanted to talk to him were his family and a few friends.

These people couldn't bring themselves to believe that he was guilty. His family was also in shock. Having just lost their beloved daughter-in-law, they were now faced with the prospect of losing their son. They simply couldn't believe that he was capable of violence.

Whelan had moved home the day after the murder and, when he was charged, decided to make the move permanent. He rented out the house in Clonard Street after having new carpets fitted and cleaning its interior.

Renting the house also helped him to save money. With no job, he had no way of paying his mortgage. There was no question of Irish Life paying out the £400,000 life insurance policy until a court had decided if he was guilty or not. Not alone was the murder a tragedy; from his own twisted perspective it was a disaster; he had accomplished nothing.

In the days following his release from Cloverhill Prison, Whelan adopted a low profile. He lived a short distance away from the Gough family home and wanted to avoid them at all costs. He was also conscious that he was surrounded by friends of his late wife.

While he could fool those who loved him; no one else was convinced of his innocence. He knew the gardaí had a watertight case that would send him to jail. This presented him with two choices. He could either stay and fight the case, or run. Knowing what evidence the gardaí were likely to produce in court, he knew the likelihood of an acquittal was slim to none. More than anything else, he didn't want the evidence of his fascination with strangulation, sex and extramarital affairs to emerge in a public forum. This would be too much.

As far as he was concerned he had no alternative but to leave Ireland and build a new life for himself. This was his only choice. Taking this action would also ensure the damning evidence against him would not emerge publicly; thereby keeping what was left of his reputation intact.

Once he made this decision, he began venturing outdoors once more. He took possession of the Peugeot car Mary bought and started visiting Drogheda and other nearby towns. Life returned to normal.

It was not long before he was seen around the local area by the Gough family, driving Mary's car. On one occasion, a member of the family saw Whelan driving the car with his window rolled down. He didn't look too worried about the pending trial. He was wearing sunglasses and looked as if he hadn't a care in the world.

But appearances can be deceptive. Whelan had a lot on his mind. He was in the throes of planning an exit strategy. While fleeing from Ireland was relatively straightforward, he knew the gardaí would go to the ends of the earth to locate him once he'd gone.

The killer also knew he would need to assume a new identity so that he wouldn't have to spend the rest of his life looking over his shoulder. First he had to decide where to go. As he didn't speak any foreign languages, this limited his travel plans. He thought up several different scenarios, before finally deciding on one that appeared to have some hope of working.

The first thing he needed was a clean passport. The killer knew there wasn't much of a chance that he could leave the jurisdiction without proper travel documents.

With this in mind, he decided to steal the identity of Martin Sweeney, one of his neighbours who lived in Gormanstown. Sweeney made a perfect victim for identity theft. He had never been in trouble in all his life; and he hadn't got a passport. More importantly Whelan knew enough about his life to impersonate him.

They were also the same age. Sweeney lived with his parents, who were considered pillars of the community in Gormanstown. Therefore, if Sweeney, or someone posing as him, applied for a passport it wouldn't arouse too much suspicion.

Sweeney had attended Whelan's wedding but the two were never friends. They were neighbours and would salute each other when passing, but that was all.

Putting his plan into action, Whelan first obtained a copy of Sweeney's birth certificate from the Births, Marriages and Death's office on Lombard Street in Dublin city. He next applied for a passport in Sweeney's name. He knew that if he were to be caught out at this point, he would face further charges, but he had nothing to lose. In his own mind, he knew he was going to prison.

But luck was on his side. As he predicted, he was issued with a passport bearing his photograph with the name Martin Sweeney. It was perfect.

Whelan never let his guard down or betrayed himself. He spent weeks meticulously planning his next move, which was to fake his own suicide. This was a key element of the conspiracy.

To make the plan work, he knew he had to make those closest to him believe that he had committed suicide because he was unable to take the torment of the upcoming murder trial. This was easier said than done.

Whelan never considered confiding in anyone, should they contact the gardaí. Instead, he started pretending to have bouts of mild depression. He engaged in this activity on an infrequent basis. He didn't overplay or underplay his angst; he just pretended to suffer from time to time.

On 12 March 2003, Whelan got out of bed and talked about driving out to Howth Head in north Dublin to pass some time.

Originally an island, Howth forms the northerly bound of the great crescent of Dublin Bay. It's cliffs are a popular destination for day-trippers from the city. Hikers make for the ancient cairn on its summit, from where they can see the Wicklow

Mountains and the city skyline. Sometimes the location is used to commit suicide. And it was for this reason that Whelan chose it.

Whelan never gave away the slightest hint that he was planning anything when he left his home that morning. The only difference about that particular day was that he didn't come home.

He did drive to Howth that morning. After parking his car in the isolated Upper Cliff Road, he left the scene making sure that no one noticed him. His only possessions were a couple of hundred euros and his new passport.

From now on he was Martin Sweeney, or later Cian Sweeney; Colin Whelan was to be no more. Before abandoning the car, he was careful to leave some of his personal belongings to make it look like he jumped from the nearby cliffs after his life had become too much to bear.

This was essential.

He then made his way to Dublin Airport. No one knows how he did this without being seen but he succeeded none the less. His disappearance was noticed that afternoon when he didn't sign on at Balbriggan Garda Station. At first, the gardaí on the murder investigation thought his car had broken down and that he'd been delayed.

Later that night, when he failed to make contact with the station, the same gardaí who charged him with murder began searching the Howth area, where they found his car.

No one on the investigation team believed for a second that he had taken his own life. However, they were obliged to search for his body on the off chance that he'd committed suicide. In the days that followed, the civil authorities mounted a major sea, air and land search but no trace of Whelan was found. By the time the authorities realised he was gone, Whelan had already boarded a flight to Spain. After checking in under the name of Martin Bernard Sweeney, the killer made directly for the departures gate and sat quietly waiting for the boarding call, counting down the minutes before he made his escape. He blended in perfectly with the rest of the holiday makers jetting off for some spring sun to the Spanish Balearic Island of Mallorca.

When he finally boarded the plane, he knew he had done it but he was too afraid to get excited, should he be arrested at the last minute.

The flight took no more than four hours. When he stepped off the plane, he was now a free man.

He walked through the airport without being stopped and caught a taxi to Puerto Portals. The resort lies nine kilometers from the centre of Palma city. It is famed for its harbour where hundreds of yachts are moored. This is where he planned to build his new life.

What made Puerto Portals attractive from Whelan's point of view was that few Irish tourists visited there. No one noticed him and he blended in well with the locals. In fact, it didn't take him long to settle in. Within days, he got a job as a barman at the plush and exclusive Squadron Bar and rented out an apartment in the nearby town of Magaluf.

There was no stopping him. He immersed himself into his new identity introducing himself as Cian; the barman, the hard-working and loveable Dubliner. He led what can only be described as a dream life on the Mediterranean Island.

He lived as if every day was his last. He worked hard, played hard and slept hard.

He gained a 'laddish' reputation among the local women while working behind the bar. Female clients were attracted to his devil may care attitude. He partied seven nights a week and enjoyed drinking sessions with other expatriates living there. It was the ultimate hedonistic lifestyle.

The town also offered him the private lifestyle he had always wanted. There was a thriving vice and lap-dancing scene in the town. Whelan was a frequent visitor to the strip clubs and availed of local prostitutes. He became a card carrying member of the Star Girls Bar, a high class lap-dancing club where performances cost €150. Whelan was given free membership of the club because he was such a good customer.

He drank heavily and occasionally used cocaine. He is reputed to have snorted coke off the bodies of prostitutes during sex sessions.

Whelan no longer had to pretend. In Spain, he could do whatever he chose.

Inevitably Whelan got involved with a woman. Her name was Katie Wilcox and she worked in O'Neill's Irish Bar in Palma Nova. Wilcox had no idea about her lover's secret violent history. She didn't even know his real name.

They starting seeing each other and, after a time, they moved into a cramped €500 a month one bedroom apartment.

This new lifestyle couldn't have been more different to his previous married life. Mary's murder was now nothing but a distant memory.

This was his fatal mistake. Although he had forgotten about the murder, people hadn't forgotten about him. While he did manage to stay out of sight at the beginning, he soon started to take risks. He became overfamiliar with his freedom.

He started drinking in Irish bars in the nearby town of Palma Nova. As time passed, he relaxed his own rules even more, often driving down to Santa Ponsa to trawl the local bars looking for women. The resort is usually full of Irish visitors. This was risky but Whelan ignored the possibility that someone would see him. This was his mistake. He lived a carefree life on the island for one year and four months until the inevitable happened. Someone recognised Cian.

~ ~ ~

Not one man on the murder investigation team ever believed that Whelan had committed suicide. His body hadn't been recovered despite exhaustive searches of the sea. While the team could never say with 100% accuracy that the tide had taken his body, their gut feeling was that he had fled, though no one could say this either publicly or officially.

The Gough family had no such legal constraints and proclaimed they had been cheated out of justice. Marie knew Whelan too well. She knew that he wasn't depressed about Mary's murder, so suicide had never been a possibility.

As far as she was concerned, Whelan was far too selfish to take his own life. In her heart, she knew that he was alive.

Nearly a year after Whelan first went missing, she gave an interview to Pat Flanagan, a reporter with *The Mirror*, insisting that her son-in-law had faked his own suicide to escape justice.

'I don't believe he's dead. He's just not the type to commit suicide. He's as hard as nails; he thinks too much of himself to take his own life. He could be anywhere for all we know. But I don't hate him; all our family wants is justice,' she said.

Marie had first heard the news that Whelan had 'disappeared' when someone rang from a newspaper to ask her to comment days after he vanished.

She knew immediately what had happened; she had always expected him to run. Inside, she was bitterly disappointed and felt she would never get justice.

She had last seen him the previous month when he had turned up at Mary's second anniversary mass. This was unexpected. At the time Whelan was charged with her murder and his appearance at the church ceremony took her family by complete surprise. In fact, everyone in attendance was taken aback by his brazenness.

Now he was free once more. Although she had tried to rebuild her life, Mary's death continued to haunt her and her family. They missed Mary terribly.

Life simply wasn't the same without her. The family didn't look forward to Christmas and other important family occasions where she would have been larger than life. From the day she died, they had vowed not to let her memory fade, nor let Whelan away with his murderous crime.

CHAPTER 10

Colin Whelan had been living as a free man in Mallorca for one year and four months when he was seen by a tourist who recognised him. The tourist knew his face from somewhere but it took him several minutes to put a name to the face. He sat in the Karma Bar and discreetly watched Cian go about his business. He listened carefully to his accent which had a north Dublin sound but he still wasn't sure.

On his return home, he immediately contacted the gardaí and told them his story. He said he'd just returned from Mallorca and had seen Colin Whelan working behind a bar.

The witness said Whelan looked slightly older and had lost some hair but he was sure it was him.

The murder team took the information and began making plans to check the accuracy of the intelligence. If it was a case of misidentification, so be it. But they had no reason to doubt the source.

In accordance with standard procedure, garda headquarters were secretly notified about the development and asked to seek the assistance of the International Criminal Police Organization, otherwise known as Interpol.

A detailed file on Whelan was dispatched to Interpol headquarters in Lyon in France, who then forwarded the file to the Spanish police.

The file included copies of Whelan's photograph and fingerprints, which would help make a positive identification.

The file said Whelan was now aged 33 but he may have changed or deliberately alerted his appearance.

The Spanish were also made fully aware about the nature of the crime he had committed. They were warned that Whelan was capable of anything, and would attempt to lie his way out of any situation. The message was received loud and clear.

In early July, plain clothes police officers started frequenting the Karma Bar. Contrary to what the gardaí suspected, Whelan had made no attempt to change his image. After spending some time watching him, they reported back that the intelligence obtained by the Garda was probably positive and they made plans to arrest the suspect later that night.

In the early hours of Saturday, 10 July, the detective team surrounded the Karma Bar which overlooks the marina and waited. Cian Sweeney was due in work at 8pm. He usually travelled on a moped which he parked outside the bar.

Regular as clockwork, Whelan arrived and parked his Peugeot 203 motor-scooter a short distance away from the bar before starting his shift that evening. He never suspected a thing. He walked into the bar and started working.

In a bizarre twist of fate, he was actually arrested while serving a pint of beer to an Irish tourist. When he was asked to step outside, he insisted that the police had the wrong man, repeatedly telling them that he was Martin Bernard Sweeney. His co-workers told the police they had made a mistake. A liar to the core, Whelan was polite and told everyone he'd be back later as he was bundled into a patrol car. He maintained his composure in case he could escape.

As he was taken away, the police began to interview his co-workers. Cian, as they called him, had been there for over a year and told them that his parents were dead. It was yet another fanciful story.

Whelan had been a good employee at the Karma, which was owned by the Squadron Bar, where he first worked. His career with the company had gone from strength to strength. In fact he had recently been promoted to head barman in charge of up to a dozen staff.

Whelan, meanwhile, continued to protest his innocence saying that he was Cian Sweeney but his body language said otherwise. He looked shocked and terrified.

When he was taken into the island's police headquarters, he was fingerprinted. The tests revealed his true identity. It was now only a matter of time before he would be flown home under the powers of the European Arrest Warrant that had been issued for his arrest when he vanished.

News of his arrest was communicated to Balbriggan Garda Station in Dublin late that night where it was greeted with delight.

Marie was next informed. She was told that Whelan would be standing trial for Mary's murder after all.

When the police made the arrest, the staff at the Karma Bar were as much stunned as Whelan. Speaking to the journalist Pat Flanagan, the bar's manager Des Mitchell said his staff members were still trying to come to terms with the fact that the head barman was a suspected killer.

'He was so polite and we trusted him totally. We can't believe he has been arrested in relation to a serious crime,' Mitchell told the journalist.

Later that night, after his identity was confirmed, Whelan was transferred to the city of Palma in Mallorca, where arrangements were made to transfer him to Madrid where he would face an extradition hearing.

It was at this point that his girlfriend Wilcox became aware that Cian was not Cian. At first she couldn't believe that Cian was in fact Colin Whelan. She had lived with him and they were building a future together. On hearing of his arrest, she travelled to Palma where she visited him in prison. As soon as she learned the truth, she ended the relationship and returned to London. She was hurt and distraught.

Back in Ireland, no one was more delighted than Marie. She had prayed each night for Whelan's arrest and had given up hope several times. When the European Extradition Warrant was introduced across Europe in 2004 she thought she would never see Whelan face justice.

'When it came into law, I said to myself, "he'll be soon gone." But I didn't lose hope. I have to say, the lads were delighted when he was found in Spain; we all were because we had been left in a limbo. To think of what he did, doesn't bear thinking about. If he had got away with it, I think it would have destroyed us all eventually,' she said.

Abandoned by Wilcox and resigned to his fate, Whelan decided not to fight the extradition order, despite initial expectations that he would do so, and volunteered to return home just thirteen days after he was first arrested.

He didn't make the decision for altruistic reasons. When he was first transferred to Madrid, he was sent to Valdemoro Prison, which houses many of Spain's most dangerous prisoners. If he had fought extradition, he would have been forced to stay in the prison for several months until his case was heard that autumn. Under Spanish law, Whelan could have then appealed against any decision by that court to send him home and the case could have dragged on for months. The thought of incarceration with the other residents of Valdemoro Prison focused his mind. Whelan was a criminal but he wasn't a man who could do time behind bars.

On the afternoon of Friday, 23 July, Whelan was brought from Valdemoro Prison to Madrid International Airport where he was handed over to two gardaí. The officers said little to him and told him they were taking him home. He didn't resist them and said nothing. He had been on the run in Spain for the past sixteen months. He had enjoyed his freedom, the sunshine and the island's women thoroughly. The three boarded an Aer Lingus flight bound for Dublin which arrived in Dublin at 9.35pm that same Friday night.

When he stepped back onto Irish soil, the first person he met was Detective Sgt Marry, one of the officers who led the murder inquiry. Whelan looked tired and gaunt. He didn't resemble himself. Gone were the smart suits and clean dress code. He was now dressed in a crumpled red t-shirt, faded black jeans and trainers with the laces removed. He looked as though he had lost weight and was very unshaven. Sgt Marry formally arrested him and took him into custody.

The next morning, Whelan appeared before the Bridewell District Court where he was remanded like a common criminal to Cloverhill Prison. He was remanded in custody 'til the following Monday when he appeared before the Central Criminal Court to fix a date for his trial.

When he came before Justice Paul Carney in the Central Criminal Court, he sat fiddling with his hands before his case was called. He had cleaned himself up. He was now dressed in a grey suit and white shirt.

The courtroom was packed to capacity. Among the crowd that had turned out to see the killer were some members of Whelan's own family. However, he did not acknowledge them or even try to make eye contact.

When the hearing began, his counsel Luan Ó Bráonáin asked the judge for a late trial date because of the 'recent publicity' his client had attracted. He said Whelan's arrest and extradition had made the front pages of the tabloids.

Ó Bráonáin was keen to make sure that his client received a fair trial, adding that the well documented events surrounding his client's arrest in Mallorca would still be fresh in the minds of a jury.

However, Justice Carney dismissed the request out of hand saying, 'This case was due to take place last October and you know perfectly well what happened.'

There was no question of Whelan getting bail, but just in case, a representative for the Chief State Solicitor said 'in these circumstances' he was seeking that Whelan be remanded in custody. The judge needed no one to tell him that bail was not on the agenda.

Though the mention of Whelan's earlier bail raised another issue. When the killer had first vanished, he had done so after his brother-in-law Jimmy Brassil had posted an independent surety of £9,900 (€12,570).

As Judge Carney remanded Whelan, he asked if any action had been taken against Brassil given that Whelan had run away. When he heard that nothing had happened, he directed that Brassil appear before the court on the following Friday to answer for Whelan's non-appearance.

Brassil appeared in court that Friday as requested. Though he had no hand, act, or part in Whelan's escape, he now found himself staring at a judge. Through his solicitor, Brassil appealed for leniency. His solicitor said Brassil had nothing to do with Whelan's disappearance and even 'organised searches' for him in the belief that he had taken his own life.

'Give him a chance, he will make a loss on this,' the solicitor pleaded. However, the judge said he had no option but to take some action.

'The credibility of the bail system requires that he suffer the loss Mr Whelan's betrayal subjected him to.'

The judge ordered Brassil to pay €1,000 for Whelan's treachery. Self-centred to the core, Whelan didn't express any emotion. He made no effort to talk to Brassil when he saw him in the court. In fact, he ignored him.

~ ~ ~

Four months after Whelan had been extradited home to face murder, he was brought one more time to the Central Criminal Court where he was confronted by Justice Carney yet again. This time his trial date was set for 11 April, the following spring.

With a well-respected and experienced legal team including Hugh Hartnett and Luan Ó Bráonáin, it seemed likely Whelan would plead not guilty but the books of evidence told a different story. The four volumes of evidence put together by investigating officers produced a damning indictment of guilt.

He knew he was not going to get out of it this time. The gardaí had uncovered every detail that was relevant to the case. They had print outs of his internet searches, more information that he compiled on how to commit the perfect murder, the email correspondence between him and Sheppard and the increased life insurance policy. There were also the various statements he made to his friends in the wake of the murder which betrayed his guilt.

Whelan knew he was a guilty man and there was no way his plea of not guilty would hold up in court. However, a plea of guilty to a murder charge is extremely rare in Ireland.

But as with everything else in his life, Whelan did the unexpected.

On the morning of Monday, 11 April, Whelan's trial began along with other murder and rape trials listed in Court 2 of the Central Criminal Court. People chosen for jury selection crammed into the over-packed court along with twenty barristers and solicitors.

A crowd of journalists from every media outlet in Ireland jostled to find standing space in the filled to capacity room. The air was stifling.

In the third and fourth bench from the judge sat Marie, her five sons with their wives and partners. They were united in their quest for justice for their beloved Mary. To the left of the Gough family sat Whelan alongside other accused murderers and rapists.

This was the first time the Gough's had come face to face with the killer since he faked his own suicide two years earlier. Whelan had dressed immaculately for the occasion, wearing a charcoal grey suit. He pretended not to see his in-laws and stared straight ahead. He showed no emotion.

At 10.45am, his barristers Hugh Hartnett and Luan Ó Bráonáin made their way through the assembled crowd. George Birmingham, the State's prosecutor, sat to the right of the court.

At the strike of 11am, Justice Carney made his way across the Round Hall in the Four Courts and into Court No 2. Listed before Whelan's trial was another trial and the Judge swore in a jury panel to try this matter. This took just a few minutes.

When a court clerk called the case of the DPP v Mr Colin Whelan, Hartnett stood up and told the judge that a 'jury was not required.'

The barrister then said it was his client's intention to plead guilty. The entire room fell silent. People stood up confused, unable to believe what they heard.

Justice Carney listened carefully and remanded Whelan in custody for sentencing the following day. This was a formality, as a guilty plea to murder means mandatory life imprisonment.

After Whelan entered his guilty plea of murder, the Gough family breathed a sigh of relief. Marie was overjoyed. Though nothing would ever bring her daughter back, she knew that Mary had finally gotten justice.

Outside Court No 2, she released a statement to the assembled media in which her family expressed their relief at the guilty plea. More than anything, she said they wanted to thank the person who reported Whelan's whereabouts to the gardaí.

'Four years ago, Mary's life was robbed from us. The hurt that she suffered will stay with us forever. We are relieved Colin Whelan has finally admitted his guilt. The last four years have been hell on earth. We have spent the time hoping and waiting for justice to be done. We would like to thank the Balbriggan gardaí and the very brave person who reported Colin to be in Spain, without which we

might never have received the justice we got today,'
the statement read.

When she went home that night, Marie felt
serene. She had a good night's sleep. In her heart,
she knew that her beloved daughter; her one special
friend could finally be at peace.

CHAPTER 11

The Gough family returned to Court No 2 the following day to witness the sentencing of the killer Colin Whelan. The courtroom was crammed to capacity with onlookers, media and Whelan's own family, who sat at the very back of the courtroom. For the two families, this part of the legal process would prove to be the most difficult. They had not known about his fascination with strangulation, or his other deviances.

This information was revealed publicly by Superintendent Tom Gallagher when he took the stand and outlined the specifics of the case. No one could have prepared Marie for what he had to say; the memory of that evidence is forever etched in her mind.

Once Gallagher was sworn in, he said he had headed up the probe with a team of officers from the National Bureau of Criminal Investigation and members of the Garda Fraud Squad.

The prosecutor Birmingham first asked him about the victim. Gallagher gave a synopsis of Mary's life. He said she had been born on 22 December 1973, and was the only girl in a family of five boys.

He said her mother, Marie, had been widowed in the 1980s. He spoke about her job and mentioned that she was highly regarded by her colleagues.

He then gave a similar description of Whelan's life. The detective said Whelan was the youngest in a family of five and was born on 14 July 1971. Much of the evidence was innocuous.

Justice Carney listened attentively. The court heard that Mary and Whelan had met in 1993 when she worked in the Huntsman. The court then began hearing the specifics of how Mary died. Her family knew she had been strangled to death but not the specifics. Nor were they aware that Whelan was a pervert who was obsessed by strangulation and murder.

As Birmingham took Gallagher through this evidence, it gradually began to dawn on Marie and her sons that Whelan had planned Mary's death for a long time; in fact long before they had even married. This sickened Marie more than anyone else. But the worse was yet to come.

Whelan sat with an expressionless face as Gallagher outlined how he trawled the internet for information on strangulation and asphyxia.

Marie listened in disbelief as Gallagher spoke about Whelan's fascination with asphyxiation, strangulation and choking. He gave details about how Whelan would search for information on the serial killer Wallace. The garda went as far as saying there were 'remarkable similarities' between the Balbriggan murder and the horrific string of murders committed by Wallace in America. He explained to a visibly shocked courtroom and Justice Carney how Wallace had kept his victims warm to disguise the time of death. He remarked that Whelan had done the same.

The evidence was stomach churning.

The history of Whelan's internet searches was something the Gough family found distressing.

Marie became visibly upset when she listened to the details of the killer's revolting internet searches as they were read into the court records. All she could think about was Mary and how she had died alone.

When Gallagher concluded his evidence, Birmingham invited Mary's twin brothers, Peter and Gerard, to address the court. In the packed courtroom, Gerard left the bench where he was sitting with his family, passing by Whelan who sat facing the floor with his head bowed down.

The atmosphere was charged.

'Our sister was brutally murdered,' he said looking at Whelan.

'Mary was the heart of our family, especially since our father died in 1989, she lifted our spirits at that time. She was very good to our mother and was a sister that my mother never had, they confided in each other. And for my mother, this is a double loss. She has lost her friend, sister and daughter.'

Fighting back the tears, he said, 'Mary's birthday is at Christmas and she really loved Christmas, it was a great family celebration when she brought everyone together. Since her death, I can't stand Christmas, she was the life and spirit of Christmas and now it means nothing to me. It's just a reminder of our family's loss and we'll never get over it.

'Our family is living a life sentence since her murder and we'll always have to live with it. We won't get off for good behaviour. Mary is gone forever and we can't run away, Mary won't be coming back.'

Now Peter directly addressed Whelan. The cowardly killer sat motionless with his eyes fixed firmly on the floor. He hadn't got the nerve to make eye contact now that the truth was known.

'We'll never, ever, ever forgive you. We all love Mary very, very, very much and my mother had great dreams for Mary's future. Mary was a beautiful girl, funny, intelligent, easy-going and straight talking. These qualities we miss so much and will miss for the rest of our lives.'

He looked straight at Whelan once more.

'On 1 March 2001, you Colin Whelan, you strangled Mary and for that we'll never, ever, ever forgive you. You caused devastation to our family when you brutally strangled Mary, and you took a piece of us too. Then you fled the country which shows you for the coward you are. You tried to rob us of justice, you thought you were above the law but you are not. Justice has finally been done here today. Mary's only crime was loving you too much. No time in prison will ever be enough. The one thing you can't take away is the wonderful cherished memories of Mary and the wonderful part she played in our lives.'

He ended his speech at that point and walked back to his seat. True to form, Whelan never said a word, showed any expression of remorse, or even got upset. He just sat there with an expressionless face.

Hartnett next stood to his feet and expressed his client's profuse apologies to the Gough family.

'He knew that what he had done was abhorrent in the eyes of any Christian,' the barrister said, adding that Whelan had expressed his sorrow 'for taking Mary away from her family.'

Hartnett then read out a note that Whelan had written. It was the first time since the murder that he had openly confessed to the murder.

The note read, 'I know these words will ring hollow for Mary's family. I will live with this regret and sorrow for the rest of my life. There are no words to explain my act.'

Part of the note was written for Marie. This part read, 'I apologise for the protracted delay today and I apologise for taking your daughter, friend and soul mate so unnecessarily.'

His sudden remorse fooled no one familiar with the tragedy. Whelan had pleaded guilty at the last moment when he was left with no option. No one believed that he possessed any remorse for Mary's brutal murder.

He was now trying to garner sympathy and protect what remained of his reputation. Marie and her family knew him too well. As far as they were concerned, his only regret was being caught.

Standing in the court and waiting to be sentenced, he looked pathetic. When the judge began to deliver his sentence, Whelan stood to his feet and lowered his head.

Justice Carney also saw through his false act of contrition. Speaking directly to the ruthless killer, the learned judge said Whelan had prolonged the suffering of the Gough family by refusing the offer of a quick trial when extradited.

More so, he remarked that the murder of Mary was 'the most calculated and callous killing' he had ever witnessed in his career, which spanned over 40 years.

In normal circumstances, he said he would backdate sentences to account for the period an accused man had spent in custody. But he refused to grant Whelan this privilege because he had absconded from the State.

The judge had not a positive word to say. He criticised him in every possible way. He noted that he had offered Whelan an immediate trial after he was first extradited but the accused had declined so a jury might forget that he had fled to Spain. This, the judge said, had 'prolonged the suffering of Mary's family and prevented any closure.' Imposing the most severe sentence available to him, he gave Whelan a mandatory life term, commencing from the previous day.

The Gough family sighed with relief and exchanged hugs as Justice Carney delivered his sentence. Justice had been served.

~ ~ ~

The killer Whelan never said a word. He was taken from Court No 2 in handcuffs to a holding cell underneath the Round Hall. There he waited to be brought back to Cloverhill Prison.

He was taken from the Four Court's Complex an hour later to begin his life sentence. The guards took him out into Chancery Street where he was mobbed by the media. When he appeared, photographers and camera men jostled for the best vantage point as he was led to the prison van, each one vying to get the best photograph of the convicted wife killer. This was his last time to see the outside world. He was now a lifer; a man who would spend the rest of his life in jail. And with that, he stepped into the prison van, the prison officers shut the door behind him and he was gone forever.

CHAPTER 12

Colin Whelan is now a model prisoner and works in the kitchen of Cloverhill Prison. A job in the kitchens is a 'dream job' for a prisoner, as they are allowed out of their cell for 12 hours of every day. Whelan usually starts his day in the kitchen at 7.30am and continues until 7.30pm.

In the morning he helps prepare breakfast for the inmates; then he has a break before beginning the lunch preparations. Then he has another break before helping to make the tea. He gets paid €47 a month. If he is lucky, he will be released in 2019. He will be 47-years-old.

He is the only Irish man ever known to have copied the murderous activities of an American serial killer. Few Irish killers, particularly husbands, methodically plan out the murders. Even fewer show the brutal ruthlessness that Whelan showed when he wrapped a towel around his wife's neck and then calmly strangled her to death without compassion.

Whelan didn't just turn into a monster overnight. After he was convicted for the horrific murder; the full details about his past history emerged.

Although Mary had never seen his ruthless side; it is now known that it certainly existed. He had brutalised and tortured women before. He had also liked to pretend to strangle his girlfriends while having sex. This partly explains his sinister fascination with the serial killer Wallace and how he perfected asphyxiation.

Before Whelan started his seven year relationship with Mary, he had previously dated a 23-year-old girl from Drogheda in Co. Louth when he was aged just 18. The two had met at local disco and her name was Helena Whitehouse.

He made her and other women feel they were beautiful and cherished. He fooled them with his faux gentleman mannerisms and then once they had fallen for him he would begin to wield his twisted and sick urges. He at first became controlling, domineering and jealous. After a time, he would insist on women obeying his sexual preferences. These were dangerous; he liked to inflict pain on young, naïve girls who fell for his seductive ways.

When Whelan was convicted of murder, Whitehouse was approached by Valerie Hanley, a journalist with *Ireland on Sunday*. She told the journalist how Whelan was a depraved and predatory monster who once strangled her with a ribbon while they made love. Whitehouse said she now believes the killer was actually trying out the technique he used eight years later to kill his young wife.

'He was into kinky sex and he would tie my legs and hands to the bed,' she told Hanley. 'He put a black ribbon around my neck and he pulled the ribbon so tight I was blue in the face and panting for breath. One night I told him I could not handle the kinky sex any more and that he was scaring me. He said that anything he wanted to do, he would do, whether I wanted to or not.'

Whitehouse later left Ireland to escape Whelan after a nightmarish relationship. While they were together, he tried to force her to have a DIY abortion and subjected her to unspeakable violence.

She actually lost his baby after he beat her up while she was two months pregnant. He had previously tried to force feed her aspirin and a bottle of vodka to induce an abortion. When that didn't work, he attempted to run her off the road, and finally he attacked her so viciously that it may have resulted in a miscarriage.

Whelan was always a highly disturbed and violent man.

When Whitehouse first fell for Whelan, she thought he was the ideal man.

'He was my first real boyfriend. Colin was attentive. He gave me flowers, perfume and a lovely chain for my neck,' she told Hanley.

But Whelan soon changed.

'After a few months he started telling me what to wear and I couldn't even look at another man. When we went out and met my friends, he would always want to go somewhere else. If I was out and met him, he would call me a tramp and other names in front of people.'

Whelan drank heavily and would subject her to physical violence. He would punch her and afterwards say he was sorry and she would forgive him. This violent psychosis intensified when she told him that she was expecting his baby. He had already made it clear that there could be no future for them if she had a baby.

'He told me to get rid of it because he didn't want his family to know anything about it. He was roaring and screaming at me,' she said.

A few days later, Whelan turned up at her flat with a bottle of vodka and a packet of aspirin. He forced her to drink the vodka.

'When I was pregnant, I went from nine stone to seven stone. I was losing weight and I wouldn't tell anyone about Colin. One night we were coming back to the flat and we were arguing. He pulled me down some steel steps and when we got into the flat, he pushed me into the front room. He got my hair and pulled my head back and with his knee thumped me into the stomach. The next day I had a miscarriage,' she recalled.

After she reported what had happened, Whelan warned her to keep looking over her shoulder. She was now terrified and moved to England where she made a new life for herself and is now happily married.

She told Hanley that she's still hurting.

'I feel like an abused child. It haunts you and it is always in the back of your head what happened. He is evil and he was born evil and I think God was looking on me and that it was for the best that I did not have Colin Whelan's child.'

Shortly after Whelan was charged with Mary's murder, Marie remembered that a school friend had tried to warn her off Whelan saying what had happened to Helena Whitehouse.

'She was warning Mary; the girl even got out of the car one night and created a scene. She was warning Mary not to have anything to do with him. But Colin said, "She's jealous, she wanted to go out with me and I wouldn't go with her."'

Whelan always posed a threat to the women he was involved with. Some members of the murder investigation believe that Whelan's motive was not to claim the £400,000 life insurance policy. These officers believe Whelan killed because he simply wanted to enjoy the sensation of strangling someone to death. Money was not the main motivation. He was just a dangerous killer who wanted to know if he could strangle someone. The payout would have been just a side benefit.

Irish Life did not pay out on policy number 6317584 issued to Whelan and his wife Mary.

Whelan will never receive any payment from Irish Life now that he was found guilty, though he continued to pay the premiums by direct debit even after he became a suspect.

Mary's mother Marie has slowly rebuilt her life. She is a truly remarkable woman. There is no question that Marie desperately misses Mary but she feels that she got justice, not revenge, in the end.

Nor does she hate Whelan. In fact she would have no difficulty meeting him to hear a face-to-face apology. She says that if he ever wants to genuinely apologise properly to her, she will meet him.

'He doesn't bother me. I'm not afraid of him. I have nothing to be sorry for. I won't shout and roar or do anything like that. I feel like a load has been taken off my shoulders, that weight, four years of living hell and trying to keep everyone together.'

She knows what it is like to lose someone precious to a killer. Mary meant the world to her. She was her best friend, her companion, her confidante and her only daughter. She cherishes the memories of the times they spent together. Marie remembers the conversations they had but she remembers the special friendship they shared most of all. She knows inside her heart that she has done everything humanly possible to keep her daughter's memory alive. She also knows that many families never get to see the killers of their loved ones face justice. Many murders go unsolved. It is her belief in justice that enabled her to survive the nightmare. Whelan is now irrelevant. He means nothing to her anymore.

'I have closure now and justice; that's all I wanted and that's all I could give Mary. We were lucky really because so many people don't get the chance.'

IF YOU'RE NOT IN BED BY 10, COME HOME

by Martin Bengtsson

Martin Bengtsson's story contains all the ingredients of best-selling fiction – murder, intrigue, sex, royalty, and espionage. And yet it is all true.

Having started out as a bank clerk, he soon made his escape and began smuggling cigarettes for the Mafia along the Mediterranean coastline.

Among many subsequent adventures – some legal, some not so legal – he worked as a bodyguard for a Saudi Arabian prince, partied with Errol Flynn and Gracie Fields, was part of a CIA hit squad and smuggled guns for African rebels.

His story has many threads which are sewn together in a wonderful narrative impossible to replicate.

Bengtsson's voice – witty, debonair and emphatically non-conformist – sings from the pages, whether he is describing his career as a stuntman on Spaghetti Westerns, or revealing his secret life as an MI5 spy.

Looking back, he says he was never motivated by politics or patriotism. 'I can honestly say I did it for the money.'

CINDERELLA MAN

by Michael C. Delisa

**Now the subject of a Major
Motion Picture starring Russell Crowe**

In 1934, in the depths of the Great Depression, a failed boxer with broken hands came off the welfare rolls for one more fight to feed his wife and three children. Four bouts later, one of the bravest men ever to step into a ring was the heavyweight champion of the world, in the greatest comeback in sports history. Jim Braddock became the 'Cinderella Man,' and inspired a troubled nation.

Once he had been a contender, a top light-heavy with skill and guts, until injuries, defeats and the aftershock of the Wall Street Crash left him toiling in railway yards and on New Jersey's Hudson River docks to pay the rent.

But one man never lost faith: his manager, Joe Gould. The tiny, loquacious Jew and the tall, straight-talking Irishman made an odd but inseparable couple, and their belief in each other was unshakable, even when Braddock entered the ring a 10-1 underdog against feared champion Max Baer, who had been blamed for the deaths of two men in the ring. How the family man with a simple cause triumphed over overwhelming odds became the stuff of legend.

WELCOME TO HELL

AN IRISHMAN'S FIGHT FOR LIFE INSIDE THE BANGKOK HILTON

by Colin Martin

Written from his cell and smuggled out page by page, Colin Martin's autobiography chronicles an innocent man's struggle to survive inside one of the world's most dangerous prisons.

After being swindled out of a fortune, Martin was let down by the hopelessly corrupt Thai police. Forced to rely upon his own resources, he tracked down the man who conned him and, drawn into a fight, accidentally stabbed and killed that man's bodyguard.

Martin was arrested, denied a fair trial, convicted of murder and thrown into prison—where he remained for eight years.

Honest and often disturbing—but told with a surprising humour—*Welcome to Hell* is the remarkable story of how Martin was denied justice again and again.

In his extraordinary account, he describes the swindle, his arrest and vicious torture by police, the unfair trial, and the eight years of brutality and squalor he was forced to endure.

DRUG LORDS

THE RISE AND FALL OF THE CALI CARTEL

by Ron Chepesiuk

Drug Lords charts the spectacular rise and fall of the Cali cartel, the richest drug trafficking gang the world has ever seen. Based in the Colombian city of Cali, it flooded the United States and Europe with cocaine, made tens of billions in illicit profits, and waged a bloody war with Pablo Escobar's Medellin cartel, leaving hundreds dead or maimed.

Led by four men - brilliant strategist Gilberto Rodriguez, his hands-on brother Miguel, the tough and vicious Jose Santacruz and the cool, dapper Pacho Herrera - the cartel seized control of the coke trade in New York in the late 1970s and used it to springboard to near-global domination. Operating like a multinational corporation, it brought a unique degree of organisation to the drugs trade and remained virtually untouchable for twenty years.

In a tale more shocking than any thriller, author Ron Chepesiuk reveals how the gang built an army of dealers, smugglers, money launderers, lawyers and assassins, and how it corrupted politicians, cops and judges. Eventually, however, its godfathers became the prime target for the U.S.-led War on Drugs, and were cut down or captured one by one.

SURVIVOR

MEMOIRS OF A PROSTITUTE

by Martina Keogh

with Jean Harrington

Survivor is the true story of a woman who started in prostitution when she was just 8 years old. Martina Keogh progressed from a brothel on Benburb Street to sporadic bouts of prostitution in St. Stephen's Green and the Phoenix Park.

When Martina was 15 she moved to the red-light district of Dublin where she sold her body for more than 30 years. This book details the problems the prostitute encounters with the police, the pimps, the punters and the public. It horrifies the reader as it reveals the violence she suffered on the streets: the weekly rapes, beatings and attempted murders.

Survivor reveals for the first time how prostitution works; the money involved, the seediness, the glamour and the good times.

IN FEAR OF HER LIFE

THE TRUE STORY OF A VIOLENT MARRIAGE

by Frances Smith

with Erin McCafferty

Frances Smith lived in Fear of her life for 22 years. Married at 16 to a Dublin criminal, she endured years of relentless mental and physical torture until she found the strength to fight back. This is her courageous story told with brutal honesty and, at times, humour. It chronicles her descent to the brink of suicide and consequent rebuilding of her life.

This unique account is essential reading for all those who have ever endured cruelty at the hands of a man or another human being for that matter. It gives hope to all those who have been victimised.

One day she found the courage to change the locks, seek a divorce and let his mistress have him for keeps. It was then that she realised he meant the vows he took on his wedding day - 'Till Death do us Part...'

The names and identities of the characters in the book have been changed to protect the author who still lives in daily terror.

SIEGE AT JADOTVILLE

THE IRISH ARMY'S FORGOTTEN BATTLE

by Declan Power

The Irish soldier has never been a stranger to fighting the enemy with the odds stacked against him. The notion of charging into adversity has been a cherished part of Ireland's military history.

In September 1961 another chapter should have been written into the annals, but it is a tale that lay shrouded in dust for years.

The men of A Company, 35th Irish Infantry Battalion, arrived in the Congo as a UN contingent to help keep the peace. For many it would be their first trip outside their native shores. Some of the troops were teenage boys, their army-issue hobnailed boots still unbroken. Others were experienced professional soldiers, but were still not prepared for the action that was to take place.

A Company found themselves tasked with protecting the European population at Jadotville, a small mining town in the southern Congolese province of Katanga. It fell to them to try and protect people who later turned on them. On 13 September 1961, the bright morning air was shattered by the sound of automatic gunfire.

This was to be no Srebrenica, though cut off and surrounded, the men of Jadotville held their ground and fought...

MORE NON-FICTION BY MAVERICK HOUSE

BLACK OPERATIONS

THE SECRET WAR AGAINST THE REAL IRA

by John Mooney and Michael O'Toole

Black Operations is the acclaimed bestseller on the Real IRA and the Omagh bombing. For the first time, the top secret world of Irish espionage and spying is revealed. From bugging stolen cars to paying off Dublin gangsters with hard cash, the authors expose the covert and often ruthless tactics used by Garda Special Branch to ensnare key Real IRA activists.

Packed with new information, Black Operations names the masterminds behind the 1998 Omagh bombing and rocket attack on the London headquarters of M16. Mooney and O'Toole also tell how Victor Barker, the father of a 12-year-old schoolboy murdered in the Omagh bombing, secretly met the Real IRA in a bid to persuade them to abandon violence.

Fully revised and updated, Black Operations also names the Dublin criminal who betrayed the republican movement to help save the Peace Process. When first published, Black Operations caused a major political storm. The Irish government was forced to admit it held face to face talks with IRA godfather Michael McKevitt - talks which the Taoiseach previous denied.

THE IRISH BALLERINA

by Monica Loughman

with Jean Harrington

Monica Loughman's story is the enchanting tale of a 14-year-old girl leaving her family in Dublin to train in a strict Russian ballet school. She brought her dreams of becoming a professional ballerina with her. While many young ballerinas' aspirations are unfulfilled, Loughman became Ireland's success story and was the first Western European to join the distinguished Perm State Theatre of Opera and Ballet.

Not just for ballet lovers, this gripping tale also details the endurance and stamina needed to survive in post Soviet-Union Russia. Set in Perm, Russia, this book weaves a tale that belongs to the finest fiction.

It evokes the closed and foreign world of ballet with natural assurance. The Irish Ballerina is the story of a young girl's single-minded determination to succeed against the odds. It is a truly engrossing story.